Grains of Truth

KAYE GIULIANI

Copyright © 2012 Kaye Giuliani

All rights reserved.

ISBN: 1479188778
ISBN-13: 978-1479188772

DEDICATION

This book is dedicated to Joanie Jenkins who invited
Proof Finders Paranormal Investigations into the
Frederick Granary and captivated my imagination with
her beauty, dedication and generosity of spirit.

CONTENTS

	Acknowledgments	i
1	Wake Up Human	Pg #1
2	A Woman's Work	Pg #7
3	Ghost Dancing	Pg #10
4	Being Catty	Pg14 #
5	Enter Arthur Fentis	Pg #18
6	Who Are You?	Pg #22
7	White Carriage From the Village	Pg #28
8	The Dream	Pg #34
9	The Right Question	Pg #37
10	Rent Please?	Pg #41
11	Silly Girl	Pg#46
12	The Fall	Pg#50
13	Where Has She Gone?	Pg#56

14	Can You Keep It Down Up There?	Pg#59
15	Stretcher On The Stairs	Pg#63
16	Dancing With Josiah	Pg#68
17	The Sign	Pg#73
18	Can I Call Anyone?	Pg#77
19	The Sentinel	Pg#84
20	Flowers from Fentis	Pg#88
21	An Alteration in Plans	Pg#95
22	Return of the Messenger	Pg#100
23	Not One, But Two	Pg#106
24	Released at Last	Pg#110
25	Ghost Adventures	Pg#115
26	Patience is a Virtue	Pg#120
27	Getting Down to Business	Pg#125
28	Face-to-Face With Dangling Will	Pg#129
29	K2 Session	Pg#134
30	When They Speak	Pg#140
31	Josiah Returns	Pg#144
32	Snoopy Dog	Pg#148
33	Welcome Home	Pg#154

34	Anxious to Share	Pg#159
35	The "Reveal"	Pg#164
36	Hello?	Pg#171
37	The Poufy Shirt	Pg#175
38	Bad Casting	Pg#181
39	Raising the Roof	Pg#186
40	Green-Eyed Ghost	Pg#193
41	I See Dead People	Pg#196
42	Project Forgiveness	Pg#202
43	He Loves Me. He Loves Me Not	Pg#207
44	Guardian and Protector	Pg#211
45	The Morning After	Pg#216
46	Wedding Plans	Pg#220
47	Payment in Full	Pg#225
48	Why Now?	Pg#230
49	Crying Over Spilled Milk	Pg#234
50	Long Time, No See	Pg#239
51	Scared Out Of His Mind	Pg#244
52	The Wedding That Set a Spirit Free	Pg#253
53	Josiah Gets There First	Pg#260

54	A Time for Celebration	Pg#265
55	A Haunting Woman	Pg#272
56	Gift Exchange	Pg#277
57	Time to Wake Up	Pg#283
58	Hello Again	Pg#287
59	A Fork in the Road	Pg#291

ACKNOWLEDGMENTS

My courage and support, as always, I owe to my friend and co-worker, Kathy Parr. Every storyteller needs to have someone on hand who is dying to find out what will happen next, and willing to believe that you have some idea.

1 WAKE UP HUMAN

In the cluttered room, a woman slept. Her hair cascaded to the right and left of her face and down the sides of her pillow like ribbons of brown silk with scattered strands of silver woven in to catch the light. The room was a fortress with battlements of carefully-stacked objects looming from every side. Mortared with dust and urine, these cast-off items had sacrificed their identities long ago to become one with the chaos. An intruder (and there had been many) could wander for hours in this world-within-a-world without ever once stumbling upon her, and she liked it that way.

A king-sized mattress and box spring sat on the floor in the center of the room. It was draped, incongruously, with an expensive ruby coverlet, delicately embroidered with vines of gold. In this setting, the bed was stunningly beautiful; a diamond set into dark clumps of kitty litter; a monarch butterfly perched atop a cow patty. On the wall behind it hung paintings of all sizes by many different artists; each one haunting in its own way; every one, a portrait of her.

Unnoticed, a perfectly round tabby cat crouched to pee in a pile of discarded clothing. He gave the sodden stuff a few good kicks with his hind legs and then made an impossible leap into bed with his human. It was time to get up. The food dishes were empty. The bowls of stale water were coated with dust and a peppering of stray hairs. He could catch a mouse, sure, but the stuff the human put down was easier to deal with, rich and oily, and very tasty.

As cats will do when it is time to get up, the tabby patted repeatedly at the human's face with all of its claws sheathed. When her eyes came open, he began to purr outrageously and butt his head against her shoulder and neck until she sat up and stretched her arms and yawned. Making sure she was watching, he ran stiff-legged (belly swinging) to sniff significantly at the empty dish before turning to stare balefully back at her.

"Good morning, Tiger Boy. Are you hungry? Okay. I'll get your food after I've had a chance to clean up a bit."

Justine Fournier slipped free of her tangled covers and stood up. A self-appointed regent, she wore her nudity as some might wear a designer gown. She moved gracefully, like the dancer she had been in her youth – without shame. In the tiny bathroom, she relieved her bladder, patted herself dry, and reached into the shower stall to turn on the water. The plumbing banged twice before spurting a few bursts of atomized water into the air. Justine waited for the rusty water to flow clear and cold before stepping in. The sliver of soap she picked up was no longer white, and had a brownish crack running through the middle where it had been wet and dried repeatedly. But, the soap still lathered generously between her palms and Justine wasn't one to waste such things. She turned to face away from the spray of metallic-smelling water and leaned her head backwards into it as her hands smoothed lather over her breasts and past the gentle curve of her tummy. The same sliver of soap provided the rich lather that she worked through her hair.

Her kingdom, this dark warren of cavernous rooms, echoed with history, immeasurable silence, and the heavy musk of cat pee. It surrounded her, and dwarfed her and, yes, protected her. These walls had been built hundreds of years ago out of stones from a local quarry. The floors had been fashioned from massive, rough-hewn lumber that didn't squeak underfoot the way much younger homes had been known to do. Rooms opened onto rooms that opened onto more rooms. 16,000 square feet of magic and mystery and stink made up Justine's world, and it was hers alone to wander through and wonder at.

In the beginning, it had been the two of them; an artist and his model with grand plans and just enough money to make them a reality. The abandoned granary had embraced them like old friends from the very start, and the work had seemed so doable and the costs of renovation so reasonable. Together, they had worked, night and day, to bring their dream to life. With love and laughter they painted, hammered and swept.

The lovers had envisioned a haven for artists; a massive gallery to showcase paintings and sketches; and dozens of private studios in which to create those masterpieces. Musicians would gather to fill it with the sounds of inspiration and joyous expression that would give rise to the Van Gogh's and Matisse's of our time. From around the world they would come – a pilgrimage of all the most gifted and talented, seeking knowledge and revelation.

But, that was before; when they were two...

Rinsing the suds from her waist-length hair, she felt the building around her like a heavy cloak. It was her home, now. She knew that people had lost their lives in this building; some of those, by choice. There was more work than any one person could complete in a lifetime, but it was her lifetime to do with as she pleased, and this work would continue until she breathed her last. She believed that her lover's spirit looked upon her labors with pleasure, and that was enough. Stepping from the shower stall, a 52-year old Justine smiled the sweet smile of a much younger woman in love.

She pulled one of Gabriel's shirts from the rolling garment pole that still served as her closet. It was the deep blue one, the one that had matched his eyes. She gathered it up and held it against her face, even though the smell of him had long since washed away. The shirt was worn and faded now. There was a small rip at the elbow and a stain at the hem, but Justine wore it with pride.

Her legs and buttocks were lithe and firm as she slipped into a pair of jeans that zipped without protest. Other women grew fat as they aged, but she had not. Her body was rarely at rest. There was money to be made by cooking and sewing; money that would bring this building back to life and fill it to overflowing with the hopes and dreams of those who were still young enough to have them. And, when that work was done, there was the hammering, sawing, painting, hauling. . .

2 A WOMAN'S WORK

In the near darkness of the early morning, Justine floated down flights of rickety stairs with nary a stumble. Every inch of this world was as familiar to her as her own reflection. On the ground floor, she had set up a studio for sewing and alterations that consisted of a heavy-duty sewing machine with such threads and notions as she required arranged haphazardly about the space. It was the sewing that paid her bills and helped her to continue the work.

A large basement area had been leased out to an Antiques dealer for so much a month, and she made a few dollars preparing modest meals for those who wished to stop by and read quietly or play board games at an eclectic mix of tables and chairs that she lovingly referred to as "the café." Here, people would pay whatever they wished for the food – some paying more than it was worth, and others paying nothing. This served the dual purposes of exempting her from the stringent laws and restrictions that Maryland required of eating establishments, and creating balance in a world that had largely abandoned the concept.

There were dishes to wash, tables to wipe down, floors to sweep and mop, and endless meals to prepare. There were late nights at her sewing machine, perfecting wedding dresses, and slipcovers and all manner of clothing and accessories; the hum of the machine the only sound; a cat in her lap; another at her feet.

On the coldest nights, though her building was not heated, she invited the homeless in to find refuge from the wind, rain or snow. She provided food, drink, old quilts and discarded sofas on which to sleep. That Justine never felt endangered doing this; and never hesitated to share what little she had, astounded her friends and family members. But, Justine was Justine.

She was a believer; a dreamer of dreams. And, in her world, everyone was created equal.

When she had money, her laundry was done at the Laundromat down the street. When she didn't, it was washed out in the kitchen sink and hung to dry on a line on the third floor. The windows up there hadn't had panes in them for years, so there was almost always a brisk enough breeze cutting through to dry things. In the winter, she would tape heavy trash bags across all of the windows (those with glass and without) in an effort to keep warm. A space heater positioned perilously close to her flammable piles and stacks of this-and-that had often made the difference between life and death, but could just as easily have set the whole place alight.

3 GHOST DANCING

Justine had just finished her sewing for the night, and had carefully laid her project aside, when he had touched her for the first time. Music had been drifting in from the next room, and she had playfully risen to embrace an imaginary partner and begun to dance.

Then, suddenly, she had stopped in mid-stride and whirled to look behind her. *What was that?*

Her breath wrapped around her heart so tightly that neither could budge. *Had someone just tapped her on the shoulder? Had she only imagined it?*

"Who's there?" Her voice sounded out of place

in the empty building, and she immediately felt silly.

After all, she was alone, wasn't she? And, even if she had been touched by a ghost, the taps had been very polite; probably just some lonely spirit requesting a turn with her on the dance floor.

Sure. Why should I be the only one who loves to dance around the house at night like an idiot?

"Is anybody there? Do you want to dance with me? Is that what you want? Hello?"

Justine had known about the ghosts for some time. There had been other instances – small in comparison. But, she had never actually been touched before.

"It's okay. I know you live here, too." She forced herself to sit down by one of the café tables and look relaxed. "I'm just. . . well. . .I wasn't expecting you to touch me, that's all. You really startled me!" She forced a nervous laugh.

Justine scanned the room for anything unusual, but only found two cats having a bath at the base of the stairs. Inky's hind leg was extended way above her head as she addressed the small patches of white fur on her tummy, and Tiger-Boy (modest by comparison) was sitting sedately on the lowest step licking delicately on a front paw. She smiled. Cats had a gift for relaxation that she would be wise to emulate

Without realizing it, her hand found the spot on her shoulder where she had been touched and rested there. She sighed deeply and got to her feet. It had been a very long day, and she had a good book waiting on her nightstand.

On an impulse, she said, "Good night, Ghostie!" as she switched off the lights.

A deep male voice breathed a "Good night." into Justine's neck that sent goose bumps running up and down her body. This time, she was rooted to the spot – afraid to turn around.

Okay. That did it. I'm out of here.

It was only a three-block walk to the nearest tavern. By the time she'd cleared the first corner, Justine had begun to feel better. It was a chilly spring night, and the fresh air was bracing. She could see the light from the tavern spilling out onto the sidewalk and hear muted strains of music long before she arrived, and they pulled her along. It was only 10:00 p.m., so occasional cars still drove along the main road to baptize her in their headlights. Anyone watching closely might have seen two shadows outlined in those beams; the shadows of a man and woman out strolling together on a clear spring night.

4 BEING CATTY

Days and weeks flew by at the defunct granary. Sometimes, it seemed to Justine as though nothing had happened that night in her sewing room. The odd occurrence of ghostly footsteps, or overturned objects was taken in stride, and life went on.

A cat showed up at the café door one night looking hungry and disheveled. He was ushered in, named "Sir Frederick" and had, to my knowledge, never missed another meal.

Justine loved his caramel-colored fur and golden eyes. Tiger–Boy protested, only mildly, as he was rather too fat to engage the new male in any kind of physical combat. Besides, they had plenty of room in which to avoid each other, and there was no shortage of food. In a matter of weeks they were scarfing up café-leftovers side-by-side in comparative peace.

Inky, as the resident female, was delighted with Sir Frederick, and would soon deliver a robust litter of six caramel-colored kittens for Justine to cuddle and fawn over. Additional litter boxes were positioned here and there throughout the maze, but were seldom used, and rarely emptied. As Justine's 'family' grew, so did the cloying stench of urine and feces throughout the building.

Justine would swear that she couldn't smell anything – and claimed that anyone who could was filled with a negative spirit that was better off being repelled. For her part, Justine was thrilled to be free of the mice and rats that plagued the other businesses on Main Street. Every 'Queendom' required subjects, and the cats were warm bodies and good companionship on many a cold and lonely night.

When things were missing, she could shake her head and blame the cats. When there were bangs and scrapings in the night; again, the cats. It was in this way that she was able to put one foot in front of the other --- day after day – alone in this dark world she was building for the good of all; needle and thread in one hand, hammer and nails in the other.

Justine's renovation efforts were largely "hit-and-miss." When she came upon something she couldn't handle, she would turn her focus to another task. As a result, the café restroom had been painted up to a point, and then abandoned. A broken stair had been replaced, but the handrail still lay balanced against one wall – (a cruel surprise to anyone fool enough to grab hold for support).

Her biggest success surrounded the clearing and preparation of a large space on the second floor where concerts and community gatherings could be held. In this area, the windows had been repaired, and the floor was solid, swept and free of debris. On these occasions, she block the entrance to her adjoining bedroom with additional garbage, and maybe scoot a drawer- free dresser or a torn and stained sofa – turned up on one end to discourage exploration.

She gloried in the music and laughter that brought some small part of their dream to reality. The work had been grueling, but she had accomplished this on her own, and it was each small success that had spurred her onward. Gabriel had loved the music, especially, and on these occasions she felt his presence more acutely than at any other time.

During the hot summer, when all of the children were bored and driving their parents up the wall, Justine would hold art classes in this space for a minimal fee, and surround herself with their laughter and boundless creativity. They made kites and giant papier maché masks and dancing figures that one could see leaning up against walls and mixed in amongst stacks of old clothing and furniture throughout the building -- hauntingly veiled under a thick layer of dust. A casual explorer would have to wonder why these creations had been left behind? Why were they not proudly on display in bedrooms and kitchens all over town? Were they meant to be the first exhibits of the future gallery? Or, were they gifts of fealty to the beloved Queen Regent of this shadowy world?

5 ENTER ARTHUR FENTIS

The antique store smelled like basements everywhere. The outer walls were more than a foot thick and made of quarried stone, and the space was large, but divided equally by thick square wooden beams that matched the color and grain of the floor throughout. A metal door at the very back of the room was kept locked at all times, as was a similar door in the left front corner. This was an effort to keep the building's past and its history locked away from the paying customers.

Arthur had filled the store to capacity with antique furniture. Most found his prices outlandishly high, but he was determined to stick to his guns in that regard. Many of the pieces were ornately carved with cherubs, fruit, demons, or all of the above. He had shifted some of the huge armoires over the gaping holes in the floor that would get his business closed in a hurry should any inspectors come through. Justine had promised to have them repaired months ago, but he had been so taken with her beauty and grace that he had never pushed the issue.

If he had to go to the bathroom during the day, he was also out of luck. On those occasions, he would have to lock up the store, walk around to the café entrance, and use the bathroom there. Conditions were far from ideal.

People who wandered in off the street looking for knick-knacks, toys or decorative items were sadly disappointed and didn't linger. Arthur kept one display case for Civil War uniform buttons and bullets and such, but nothing that would be of interest to the average antique browser.

In fact, Arthur Fentis spent a great deal of time sitting behind his desk in the empty, basement-smelling, store trying to ignore the sounds that emanated from the two locked doors. He knew that the one to the side hid the silo where a young boy had drowned in a sea of grain a hundred years ago after tragically falling in from the top floor. Arthur didn't hear men's voices from the stone silo, and he definitely didn't see the knob jiggling frantically every Wednesday at 3:00 p.m.

But, it was the other door. The one at the rear of the shop that was hardest to ignore. Behind that door lay the main reason that the basement had gone no further; the builders had stumbled upon the entrance to an ancient cave that had been carved into the stone by native Indians for the purpose of conducting sacred rituals. The photos had been taken and the archaeologists had done their bit, but the cave was to be kept "as is" for historical purposes, and so there it was. Behind that door.

Moans and chantings and the smell of smoke came through that door. Scratching and growling and loud bangs that drew all eyes had to be explained away with every ounce of creativity he could muster; and Arthur wasn't a creative man.

The rent was cheap and the landlord was attractive, so he remained as stoically unaware of the disturbing paranormal happenings as he was of his unreasonable prices and steadily failing business. At 5'10", with dark slicked-down hair and a dapper appearance, Arthur Fentis imagined himself next in line to be the owner / proprietor of the Granary Gallery. There were no other men in Justine's life (he was certain of that), and when she finally realized that the renovations were too much for her to handle on her own, well, he would offer his services. Definitely. All of his services.

6 WHO ARE YOU?

One night in December, when Justine was feeling particularly blue about the prospect of facing another Christmas without Gabriel, the mysterious dancing phantom made his first appearance. She had just flicked off the last light before starting up the stairs to bed when she noticed, with annoyance, that there was still light coming from the sewing room.

Darnit! I know I turned everything off in there. Sometimes I think I'm losing my ever-loving mind. . .

With sure steps she had traversed the dark café to turn off whatever it was that she had forgotten, but, having successfully navigated all of the tables and chairs, she froze in the doorway to the sewing room –

her silhouette framed in an eerie, undulating glow. For long seconds there was no sound or movement. Justine's hands fell slowly to her sides. She drew a hesitant breath.

"Well, hello." She said to the wavering image before her. "And, who might you be?"

The spirit moved closer, and Justine fought to stand her ground.

"Are you the fine gentleman who likes to dance? What is your name?" Before her eyes, the blurry figure was becoming clear and she began to make out the features of a handsome face and broad shoulders.

But, before anything else could take place between them, Sir Frederick had ambled, loose-jointedly into the room, seen the spirit, and proceeded to freak out in a major way. Every hair on his – by this time – extremely rotund body stood up. His ears flattened against his caramel-colored head and he began to hiss and spit at the glowing entity for all he was worth.

The room around her fell into an instant blackness. As anyone can imagine, the cat had done more to frighten Justine than the apparition, and her heart was racing, but she made no move to turn on the lights.

"Freddy! Stop that! You scared me to death!" She gasped to Sir Frederick's fleeing behind. His tail was at full surrender as he had taken that opportunity to pull a 'Flintstone' retreat; his four feet blurring into a sliding, skidding machine for getting-the-hell-out-of-there. She collapsed against the door jamb with a hand to her heart.

"Hello?" She whispered again into the silence. "You can come back now. He's gone. He's just a silly cat. I'm not afraid of you. . ." Then, just in case there was mind-reading involved, she added, "Well, I'm trying not to be afraid. . ."

But, the room clung to its velvety blackness, and the silence that surrounded her had that certain hush that only an empty room could convey.

"I'm going to bed, now." She said – just in case.

"I hope you'll come and see me again sometime. Maybe we could dance?"

Justine backed slowly out of the sewing room and didn't turn back around until her backside bumped the edge of the first café table. She slipped her hand into the right front pocket of her cozy, cable-knit sweater and pulled out her cell. She wanted to call someone; but who?

Her thumb found the backlight button and she scanned through her personal directory. Angela? No. Carol? No. She paused over her mother's number for only a moment before continuing on down the list.

Who do you call when you've just seen a ghost?

Justine thought about her purse hanging from a hook beneath the kitchen counter. She could step out for a few drinks? Maybe she would run into some people she knew, or strike up a conversation with people she had never met? She didn't want to be alone. Not tonight. Disturbing thoughts were assaulting her like tennis balls pitched from a machine. As each one flew at her, she would send them on their way with a determined mental 'thwack!"

What if he watches me sleep at night? What if he wants me out of the building? If he can touch my shoulder, then can he also push me down the stairs? How long has he been here? Has he watched me take showers and go to the bathroom? Can he read my mind?

But, in the end, Justine decided to be a brave girl and head upstairs to bed. Obviously, the spirit had been living in the Granary since last spring. If nothing horrible had happened in all of those months, then nothing was likely to happen now.

"Ghosts are just people who have died." She repeated to herself. "Besides, if he was all that powerful and evil, he probably wouldn't have been scared off by a silly cat!" Feeling better, a smile relaxed her face.

She climbed the rickety wooden steps in total darkness, as was her habit -- seven steps to the landing; another seven to the second floor. Halfway across the length of the 'concert hall,' she turned right through a narrow opening and made her way, expertly, through tall piles of garbage to her room.

The lights were first; mismatched and chipped, each turned on at its base. Never very bright, they gave her sanctuary a warm glow that radiated a sense of wellbeing and security. Breathing what must have been her first full breaths since the encounter, she flopped onto her bed and kicked off her shoes. Justine reclined onto her pillows without pausing to undress, and let out a heavy sigh. It had been a long day and she was tired.

For Maryland, November had been unseasonably warm, and there was no need to start up the space heater. Insulated, as she was, by all of those cast-off possessions, the room was cool, but not uncomfortably so.

The novel on her nightstand was calling to her, but the sensation of her tired arms and legs seeming to melt into the lush coverlet soon carried her off into a deep, uninterrupted sleep.

7 WHITE CARRIAGE FROM THE VILLAGE

Just days before Christmas, a young girl pushed through the café door with a cumbersome dress bag draped clumsily over her arms. She stomped the freshly-fallen snow off of her boots onto the rubber mat and looked around.

A dozen or more, strangely-dressed, patrons were digging into piles of waffles or mounds of scrambled eggs as they conversed easily with one another. One man, in particular, caught Kathy's eye. He was wearing a black wool coat that was several sizes too small and clutching a dripping waffle in both hands. A girl's red knit hat topped with a huge white pom-pom rested limply by his plate.

Not wanting to be caught staring, she lowered her eyes and was horrified to see that one of his feet was bare. Had she wandered into a homeless shelter by mistake? She shook her head, mentally comparing the address on the door with the one Alyssa had scribbled on her note pad.

This couldn't be a shop that did wedding dress alterations, could it? A woman with long, dark hair was busying herself behind the kitchen counter, and Kathy shifted her heavy bundle from right to left before stepping forward to introduce herself.

"Hello?"

The woman looked up, and Kathy couldn't help noticing how beautiful she was.

"Hi honey, you look frozen through. Can I get you some waffles this morning? They're our Tuesday special." She had smiled warmly.

"No. Thank you, though. They look. . . um. No. I was told that this was a good place to have alterations made? Am I in the wrong. . . um. . . I must be in the wrong place." Kathy's face flushed with embarrassment, and she started to turn away.

Seeming to notice her burden for the first time, the woman came around the counter quickly to take it up.

"You are absolutely in the right place!" With strong arms, the dress bag was whisked away to the next room where it was hung on a rolling clothing rack beside several others just like it.

"Hi! I'm Justine. It's a pleasure to meet you, um. . . "

"Kathy. Kathy Harold." She smiled, relieved to have her arms free at last. "My wedding is in February, and this dress isn't fitting the way I want it to. I was hoping that you could help? I know that doesn't give you much time. . . "

"No worries. I'll have it finished in plenty of time." Kathy was ushered into a small velvet-curtained enclosure to undress while Justine pulled the gown from its plastic cover and turned it this way and that. "Oh, this is lovely!" She had exclaimed. "I'll bet you're an absolute angel in this!"

Kathy sat on a battered three-legged stool to pull off her wet boots and laughed. "Would you believe it was the first dress I tried on?"

"Sure. I hear that all the time. I'm one who believes that fate plays a role in all things. Do you think that's crazy?"

"Well? That depends." Kathy smiled. "Is it fate that forced me to drag my wedding dress all the way from Montgomery Village during the season's first snow storm in my mother's broken-down van?"

An odd look passed over Justine's face that Kathy could not see. There was a pause before her reply. "Were you, by any chance, driving a white van?"

Thinking that Justine must have seen her drive by several times – looking for the correct address – Kathy said, "Yes. That was me! I couldn't figure out why I'd been given the address of a café when what I wanted was wedding alterations."

Justine paused again. "That confuses a lot of

people. Sewing is just one of the things that I do to make ends meet around here."

"Oh. Maybe you should put a sign up or something."

"Maybe I should. Kathy, go ahead and slip it on and I'll be back in a few minutes to take a look. Okay?" She said, passing the dress through a gap in the drapes.

"Will do. Thanks."

Justine returned to the kitchen just as the timer went off for the next waffle. She pulled open the iron and lifted the golden brown waffle out with a fork.

"Sticks! Your waffle is up! Hurry, now. I've got a customer in the back!"

The homeless man wiped syrupy-buttered hands on his pants and stood to claim the next waffle. Justine drew in a sharp breath as he crossed the room.

"Where's your other shoe, Sticks? You can't be walking around in the snow like that!"

"I ain't 'xactly sure. It warn't there when I woke

up this mornin'." His skeletal hand snapped up the steaming waffle and passed it quickly hand-to-hand as he shuffled back to his table.

Justine shook her head and stomped with determination off to the storage room to scoop up Gabriel's abandoned work boots. She cradled them close for a moment before turning resolutely back to the café. They'd probably be too big, but, well, maybe with some rags stuffed in the toes?

8 THE DREAM

Justine's dream was always the same. It started with the window on the fourth floor. She knew the window because it had looked out on the main road with a view that could identify travelers from far away. All day long the clatter of passing wagons signaled the deliveries of produce to the markets, mills and warehouses that made up the bustling downtown of Frederick in the late 1800's.

A scream, followed by much shouting and excitement caused the Watcher to turn from the window. It was a horrible, high-pitched scream that had choked away to nothing with an unexpected abruptness that defied understanding.

Soon there was a mantle of grief laid upon the

Watcher's shoulders, and when he turned again to look out the window, the city below had been wearing a mantle of its own; factories, cobblestones, and houses alike had been covered in a heavy blanket of snow.

Unable to endure the weight of his grief, the Watcher found a sturdy length of rope and set about making a noose in which to rest his head. The rope was made to pass over a thick beam that waited patiently above to lend its support. Not once during the cruel preparations had a carriage passed on the street below. The snow remained virginal – pure and white. The planned act seemed blessed by its silence and majestic witness.

When all had been made ready, the Watcher turned once more to gaze upon his city for the last time. The mantle of his grief dripped with the blood of the innocent and pooled at his feet. Though the high-pitched death cry was heard no more within those walls, the Watcher heard naught else. The death of his only son, drowning in the grain at the bottom of the silo, had proven to be more than he could bear. His only wish was to be carried off to join the boy in whatever lay beyond.

The noose was lowered over his head, the chair was kicked from beneath his feet, and after a brief and agonizing struggle, his spirit walked free of his mortal body and went once more to the window. But, he became confused and fearful. Where was he to go now? Where was he to find his son? The years passed like the pages of a book in a breeze, but always he stood in that window – watching.

Finally, off in the distance, a growling thunder could be heard. The Watcher's spirit searched the horizon for the source of the noise, and was treated to the sight of a great white carriage, moving through the snow without benefit of horse, or mule, or ox. When, at last, it had pulled to a stop under the window, a bright angel stepped out of it into the snow. She carried his white robes upon her arms, and, when her face looked up, their eyes met and he knew that he had been seen.

Excited now, the Watcher waited.

9 THE RIGHT QUESTION

As the woman called Justine pinned and fussed over the bodice of her gown, Kathy took in her surroundings. The outer walls were stone, and the ceilings were very high. Looking through the windows onto the street, she could see bubbles and warps in the glass that spoke of days long gone. She felt as though she had stepped through a mirror, or become caught up in a Twilight Zone episode. There was that aura of . . . she struggled to find the right word and decided on. . . "other-worldliness" about the place.

"Wow. This building is old, isn't it?"

Pins filling her mouth, Justine nodded vigorously.

"It's haunted, too. Did you know that?"

Kathy watched Justine freeze where she stood, and hoped she hadn't said the wrong thing. After a shocked pause, the woman spit the remaining pins from her mouth to her palm and raised her eyes.

"Yes. Very much so." She whispered.

"I know. I saw him." Kathy admitted, conspiratorially.

"Him?"

"Oh! Are there more, then? Cool!"

A light went on inside the lovely woman, and Kathy could almost hear the drawbridge of Justine's defenses lowering as the next words were spoken. "Would you like to see the rest of the place?"

"Are you kidding? I'd love it!" Then Kathy remembered what her mother had said about getting the van back by noon. "Oh, darn. What time is it?" A quick glance at a clock radio that was squatting on a pedestal by the door only made things worse. "Oh, no. It's almost 11:00 and I have to be heading back. Can I take a rain check?"

The woman's disappointment was clear. Maybe she really needed to talk to someone about the paranormal stuff that must be going on around her all the time. Kathy had been able to see ghosts for as long as she could remember. During her school years, she had kept such things to herself and had felt very alone, but now that she was getting married and coming into her own, she saw no reason to deny the gift she had been given. Thankfully, her fiancée shared the same abilities. It had been such a relief to find a man who could truly understand and accept her the way she was.

"Maybe I can do the tour when I come back to pick up my dress? When do you think it will be ready?" She asked, hopefully.

"Oh. It won't take more than a few days. I'll give you a call when it's ready and we can work something out."

"That would be great! Um. . ."

"What?"

"Would you mind if I brought my fiancée with me? He could wait in the café while I try on the dress and all that, but. . ."

"Yes?"

"Well, we are both able to see things; things that other people don't."

Justine's smile was vibrant and her eyes glittered with anticipation. "There are *two* of you! Please, do come as often as you like. There are many "things" to see and hear in this old building, and I can't tell you how happy it would make me to have them seen and heard by somebody else! Before you walked in here, I was taking measurements for my own strait jacket!" She laughed.

"Then, it is a date!" Kathy confirmed. "And, we will sort these apparitions out together."

Later, back in the van and headed home, Kathy dialed Bill.

"Honey! Guess what? We've got a date with some ghosties in Frederick!"

10 RENT PLEASE?

Justine dried the last glass and set it aside. A quick survey confirmed that everything had been made ready for the breakfast rush that would come with the new dawn. Exhausted, and with some degree of irritation, she turned her attention to her uninvited audience.

"Well, Arthur, it's getting late and I have enough alterations lined up to keep me sewing until dawn, so..."

"Oh, don't worry about me.! I'm just enjoying the view. If you'd like some company while you're working, I'd be happy to hang around..."

She was fairly sure that what he was doing with his face was meant to come across as endearing, but in that, he had failed miserably. Arthur Fentin was the only person Justine had ever known who could turn her stomach. He was an oily, unattractive, self-absorbed little bougar of a man.

"Ah. That's good of you Arthur, but this kind of work requires my full attention, so . . ."

He raised his eyebrows. "Oh? Well, then I'll just be on my way." He stood and gathered his things to leave; pushing his empty mug across the counter to her. "Thanks for the coffee; best in town I've always said."

"Arthur?"

At her voice, he stopped and turned with the glint of hope shining from his eyes "Yes?"

"The rent?" She presented her palm while resting the other hand firmly on her hip.

"Oh! Yes! Of course!" He said, reaching into his suit pocket for his checkbook.

"Have you got a pen handy? I'll write you a check, this minute."

Justine gestured to the bouquet of writing instruments that bloomed from a modified mason jar by the cash register. Embarrassed at not having noticed them, he selected a pen.

"Is it the 23rd already?" He clucked, scribbling dutifully across a blank check. "How could I have left it this late? And, Christmas right around the corner. Which reminds me . . ." Arthur's eyes locked onto hers. "Do you have anything special planned for the Holidays?"

"No. Just work and more work."

Justine busied herself washing and drying his mug as he prattled on. Being late with the rent was one of Arthur's most dependable traits.

"I'm having a little Christmas Eve get together at my place. I'd love it if you could drop by for a drink or two." Signing the check with a flourish, he handed it to Justine. "Here's December's rent, and January's, too!"

Now, *that* was a surprise. She scanned the check and smiled with genuine gratitude.

"Great! Thank you, Arthur. This will come in handy."

"So, do you think you'll be able to put the drudgery aside for a few hours and join me for some Holiday cheer?"

It seemed an eternity before she was able to lock the door behind that objectionable wart. She knew that she should be grateful for the income his store provided, but would have evicted him without a second thought had another vendor come forward to take the space.

Justine leaned her back against the closed door with a heavy sigh. She knew that there were six dresses, a man's suit, and the canvas cover for a ski boat awaiting her attention. She cleared away some of the dinner tables and ended up leaving a dangerously high stack of dishes near the sink. They would have to wait.

On nights like this, she wondered what the hell she was doing with her life. Every surface on which she could rest her eyes was clamoring for attention. Tables screaming to be wiped off, floors to be swept and mopped, dishes to be washed / dried and put away; there was no end to it. Day after day after day and onward until her last day dawned. . .

Tears threatened to fall, but Justine rallied. With the flick of a switch, she was once again a silhouette in the door to her sewing room; the riotous fall of her curls a deeper shadow to her waist. With an impossibly straight back, and a palpable resolve, her arm extended to retrieve a cocooned wedding dress.

Though she had moved out of sight of the doorway, a gentle "click" could be heard, followed by a stream of big-band music that filled every corner and crevice with comforting sounds from the past.

11 SILLY GIRL

Bill listened to Kathy as she prattled excitedly about the old Granary and its ghosts. It had been such a relief to find her; someone who understood. As she talked, he could imagine the movements of her mouth and eyes; they way she swept her hair back whenever wisps fell around her face. He didn't listen to half of what she said, but had already surmised that a trip to the Granary was unavoidable. He smiled, contagiously, and tapped his pen on his desk.

As Bill saw it, ghosts were just about everywhere. You didn't have to travel to Frederick to find them. Most of the time, they just went about their business. Rarely did any spirit approach him for assistance, or engage him in conversation. As a young man, he would sometimes mistake the dead for the living – a blunder that had caused him untold misery and humiliation among his peers. The resulting strategy – to ignore everyone who wasn't immediately familiar – hadn't served him much better; giving him a reputation for being "Snooty and unapproachable."

He had met Kathy while attending the University of Maryland, Baltimore Campus. She was very open about her "gift" and he had been instantly intrigued by her popularity in spite of that. Watching her from a safe distance over the next several months, he eventually found the nerve to approach her and was instantly caught up in her enthusiasm for everything alive, dead, or in between. The connection had been instantaneous, and their ensuing engagement had come as no surprise to anyone who knew them.

"Wait until you meet this woman who lives there! She is beautiful! But, in a different way than you'd think. . . it's hard to describe, but you'll see what I mean."

"Sounds exciting. So? When are we planning to take this magical mystery tour?" He joked.

"She's going to call me as soon as the dress is ready. You know what? I think I'm going to send Michelle and Yvonne there for alterations, too. Everybody says she's the best, and I think they must be right."

Billy lost track of the conversation again. Listen to her! Like pouring a bottle of bubble bath under a running spigot, she was bubbling over with iridescent pops and sparkles – so full of love for everything and everyone. *She loves me.* He thought, feeling lucky.

Ever since the ghost of his murdered sister visited him at the age of six, Billy had known that he was different. There had never been any reason for him to doubt what he saw and heard that night, and that sure knowledge had instilled in him an unshakeable belief that spirits could walk the earth, if they chose to do so. His mother had seen Charity, too, but had been able to convince herself otherwise over the years. It was his parents, initially, who had advised him to keep his "visions" to himself. Because of that, he held his experiences in a much more private way than his new fiancée ever could. Yet, her candor and bravery never failed to impress him.

"Ooops! The roads are really slick! I almost creamed mom's van!"

"Okay. You'd better get off the phone and concentrate on getting home in one piece." He said, protectively.

"You're probably right. Will I see you tonight?"

"Yep. How about we meet at Brewer's Table at 7:00?"

"Yay! Love you! I can't wait! Bye."

He disconnected the call and slid his cell into its beat-up leather case. *Why is she driving the van instead of her new Focus?*

Billy Fische shook his head and vowed to ask her about that over dinner.

12 THE FALL

It was bound to happen, eventually. The components were all in place for that kind of thing, and even self-appointed monarchs can make the occasional misstep. Ultimately, it was Tiger Boy who took the blame, though he would profess his innocence in the way that all felines do, with some modicum of grace and an all-encompassing lack of humility.

Justine had fed the lunch crowd and was just finishing up the dishes when she heard a huge crash from somewhere upstairs. Whatever had fallen had been heavy enough to shake the massive beams under her feet, and nothing was that heavy, so she wasted no time in jumping to her feet to check things out.

The loud boom had frightened her, badly, and Justine's imagination was running wild as she hurried to find out its cause. Did the roof cave in? Did a section of flooring collapse? A set of stairs fold in on itself? Whatever it was, she was fairly certain that repairs would be extensive and costly. With her heart in her throat she checked the building floor, by floor. She experienced relief as each area she entered proved undamaged.

What the hell? She gasped as she reached the fourth floor and took in the disaster that lay before her.

One of the enormous ceiling beams had broken in half and fallen to the floor, bringing a good bit of the roof down with it. Snow was drifting in as though it was the most natural thing in the world to blanket the top floor of a granary.

She examined the fallen beam. Justine knew termite damage, and so was very happy to find none of that. No rot, either. But, what could have caused this beam to snap like a toothpick, and what was she going to do about it? She brought her hand to her forehead.

I'm going to have to call in some favors, that's for sure. Somebody has to know somebody else who can repair a 200-yr-old roof. Right?

"BANG!"

With a sudden, loud violence a trap door to the front silo slammed open.

Justine stared at it for a long time. *Okay. That can't happen. Those are heavy and haven't been opened for decades. I just saw that happen, but that can't happen.*

She inched towards the open trap door. It was one of twenty or so that made up most of the floor on this level. When it had been a working granary, the grain had been pumped into this top story so that gravity could do the lion's share of the work. After delivery, a trap door was opened, and grain was swept into the correct silo or bin for processing. Even though the closed trap doors were probably safe to walk on, Justine had always made an effort to navigate around them. She had opened one, once, and it had been a very long way down.

When she was still about two feet away from the opening, she froze. The trap door was moving. It was slowly lifting off the floor as though it were planning to . . .

"WHAM!"

Justine wasn't breathing. She hadn't seen that, because it couldn't happen. Simple.

"Hello?"

Something scraped across the floor behind her and she wheeled around to find Tiger Boy batting a chunk of building material around as though it were a mouse.

The air whooshed out of her, and she allowed herself a giggle.

"Tiger Boy! What are you doing way up here? Did you come to see what all the excitement was about?"

She reached down and scooped him up. A sudden cramping in her side caused her to gasp out loud before it lessened and faded away. She chalked it up to the three pieces of drywall she had hung the day before. She wasn't getting any younger.

Most of the cats that shared the granary with her were feral and wouldn't allow much in the way of physical contact, but Tiger Boy had been with her for years and they were old pals. He was like a plump, furry beanbag in her arms. Holding him close and listening to his purr was very calming. Whatever had just happened, it seemed to have stopped for now. Her mind began to focus on what she needed to do to get the roof patched.

And the hatches nailed shut?

Feeling much calmer now, Justine took a few steps away from the offending hatch door and carefully avoided the others between her and the stairs. She still had the cat cradled in her arms, and was relieved to note that the room had gone completely silent; the snow gently floating down to cover the fallen beam. She had made it down the first three steps of a 10-step flight when everything changed. . .

"WHAM!!!!!"

Justine started and Tiger Boy struggled out of her arms in a mad leap for safety. Her foot had been moving forward to land on the next step down, but never made it; her heel catching the rim of the step she was on and pitching her, violently, forward. There was impact after impact, and pain. Alone on the third floor of a 16,000 square foot granary, Justine lost consciousness.

13 WHERE HAS SHE GONE?

Gazing serenely down the wooden stairs at the fallen woman, he was surprised to feel remorse for his tantrum. The woman was still alive. He took a moment to contemplate how much nicer it would be if she wasn't. It was lonely business being a ghost.

He had just been so sure that the angel in the white van had seen him, and that she would come to him and . . . Well, he wasn't exactly sure what it was he had been hoping for. Answers? Direction? Hope?

Preachers had warned from many a pulpit the grim circumstances that awaited any man who took his own life. Burning eternally had seemed nothing in comparison to the agony of his grief! Visions of James' body being pulled from the silo – a broken neck and riding a flood of yellow grain. . . It was more than any loving God could have expected him to bear. Walking to work without James beside him. . . No. Death had seemed his only option; the only available release from the agony of living on.

But, standing next to his awful corpse that night, and coming to the sick realization that James was not there waiting for him. . . How much more horrible than eternal flames? Here, he was constantly reminded of his grief and stupidity. The years passed in darkness as the living passed through and around him as though he had never existed.

When the white van had rumbled away through the snow, leaving him behind again to suffer alone, all of the grief and loneliness and confusion had risen in him like a storm! The beam that had born the rope that had ended his life now bore the weight of his wrath for its role in seducing him to that end. The door that had swept his only son to his death was thrown open and slammed shut again in anger. Yes. He had seen his opportunity to really frighten the woman as she had been poised there on the stairs. . . He wanted her to know he was there! He wanted her to know he was angry! But, now she lay crumpled on the floor like a lovely porcelain doll, and he was ashamed.

How could the angel have left without coming to speak to him? How long would he have to wait until another came? Where had she gone?

A sick thought passed through him like a remembered shudder. What if this most recent transgression had sealed his fate? He had not meant to harm the woman – yet there she lay. Perhaps he could help in some way?

The troubled spirit of William James Poston hovered near Justine's crumpled form and contemplated his options.

14 CAN YOU KEEP IT DOWN UP THERE?

Arthur Fentis was closing a sale on a $6,899.00 armoire that had been sitting on his sales floor for over a year when the loud commotion started overhead.

"CRASH!"

"Oh, my! What's that? Is the building coming down?" The blue-haired shopping buddy of his customer slapped her hand across her ample bosom and craned her head towards the ceiling.

"No, no. Of course not." Arthur crooned in a soothing voice as he ushered the two women toward his cash register. "They are upstairs making some much-needed renovations."

"BOOM!!"

Everything shook. That had been a big one.

What the hell is she doing up there? She's going to chase off my customers and screw up this sale!

"Esther. I think we should go. We can come back another time. I don't think this building is. . . "

"THIS BUILDING!" Realizing that he had gotten a bit loud, Arthur lowered his voice to continue, "This building is over 200 years old, ladies. Look. The walls are quarried stone, 3ft. thick, and the beams above and below you have the circumference of the average tree! I assure you that, while noisy, the renovations upstairs need be of no concern." He twisted his face around to create his most winning smile. "Now, Mrs. Cohen, if you leave a 20% deposit on the armoire, I can arrange to have it delivered to your home any day next week. What day would be best for you?"

"BANG!"

Both women jumped and went pale. Their eyes

were wide and their mouths – painted haphazardly in garish shades of red – puckered simultaneously into shocked 'O's.

"Thank you for your help, Mr. . . . Mr. . ."

"Arthur Fentis, at your service, Madam."

"Yes. Well, Mr. Fentis. We have decided to think about this a bit more. Perhaps we will be back next week to have another look at it.

"But. . ."

The ladies clicked and hobbled over to the door as fast as their best church shoes could carry them; practically wrestling to gain exit.

"No worries!" Esther sang as she made her escape. "We'll be back another time. Thank you!"

Arthur leaned in the doorway and watched his patrons -- and his profits -- hustle away down the shoveled sidewalk. In the distance one of the ladies was heard to say, "It was too big for my bedroom, anyway. Probably best left behind."

"BOOM!!"

His eyes rolled upwards and he crossed his arms in irritation.

"Okay. That's absolutely it. I've had enough! If Justine is going to pull down walls and shake the whole building during business hours, then she had better start looking for another vendor to lease this god-forsaken, haunted, musty and miserable basement."

He stalked off towards the café entrance with every intention of taking matters sternly to hand – all the time counting the (imaginary and unrealistic) number of patrons that he would lose during his time away from the shop.

As Arthur entered the Café, there was another resonant crash from above.

15 STRETCHER ON THE STAIRS

The paramedics looked around with a sense of amazement. You knew they had to be wondering what kind of a place this was, and how they were supposed to get the stretcher up so many rickety, wooden-slat, stairs with no handrails. With two flights to each floor, the journey to the third level had seemed endless; the tight turns; the dizzying lack of risers that permitted the climbers a full view of the flights below.

The strange little man who led the way kept waving them onward. "She's up here!" He would say, "On the third floor!"

From his short, hysterical outbursts, they had gleaned that the victim was unconscious, but still breathing. Her arm was probably broken, as it had been twisted at impossible angles to the rest of her body. There was blood from a head wound that was profoundly swollen. Overall, it didn't sound good. But, they were prepared to do their standard, on-site, evaluation. She would be stabilized on a back board and transferred to the hospital with lights and sirens blazing. It was only 2:30 p.m., and this was their third transport of the day.

Ryan had been a paramedic for five years. As a more senior member of the crew, he ascended behind the stretcher bearers with the standard equipment hanging in satchels from each hand. Ryan was not particularly comfortable with heights, so he made it a point to focus on the perfectly straight back of the odd little man at the front of the queue. If ever there was a man with a stick up his. . . well. . . He let the thought slide away. He needed to stay on task and serious.

Just as the group was rounding the corner to the last flight of stairs, there was a huge, "BOOM!" that caused them all to jump and stumble.

"What the fuck was that?!" Kyle whispered,

visably shaken.

"Language, Kyle." Ryan glared at him.

"That has been happening all day." Mr. Fentis, said. "Probably wind gusts caused by the roof cave-in."

"Roof? Nobody said anything about a roof." This from Kyle; his eyes now glued to the ceiling.

"Come along!" Mr. Fentis urged. "She's just over here!"

The first thing Ryan saw was her hair. So long and thick and truly beautiful, it was splayed out around her head like a lion's mane. Then, the paramedic in him clicked on and he was kneeling beside her with his equipment bags open and his competent eyes taking in the needs of this latest patient.

"What's her name?" Ryan asked, urgently.

"Justine." Arthur answered.

"Justine? Justine? Can you hear us? We are here to help you, Justine."

As there was no response, the team got busy stabilizing her arm – which was clearly fractured – and bandaging her head wound. The blood was not as worrying as it could have been, and that was a good sign. The most troubling aspect of this case was that she had not responded at all to what must have been extremely painful repositioning of her body as they prepared it for transport. Her pupils were dilated and fixed. Coma? Ryan jumped on his Nextel.

"Transporting female, approximate age of 40, comatose, multiple fractures of the right arm, head wound."

An annoying beep followed by a short burst of static and then a reply. "Respirations? Blood pressure? Internal bleeding?"

The answers and questions flew back and forth, but it wasn't long before the team was headed back down the treacherous stairs towards the ambulance. Once again, the odd little man had taken up his position in the front. Ryan wanted to tell him to get out of their way, but decided rather quickly that there was no way to get around him in this tight space.

"Did you say 'comatose'" He was whining. "You did, didn't you?"

"Sometimes comas are a blessing, Mr. Fentis. The body shuts off unnecessary systems in order to repair the damaged ones. If she was conscious, believe me, she would be suffering a great deal."

"Oh. This is just terrible! I shall have to close down for the rest of the day! I'll put a sign on the door out front. This is a horrible turn of events! Just horrible!"

Ryan did his best to hide his annoyance. It helped to notice Mr. Fentis' unmistakable resemblance to the Rabbit in *Alice in Wonderland*. Finally free of the man, they loaded Justine into the back of the ambulance and turned all of their attention towards accomplishing her safe transport to the hospital.

16 DANCING WITH JOSIAH

Justine was dancing. Surrounded in mist with no floor beneath her feet, she was whirling about in the arms of a most-competent lead. She felt as though she could dance forever, without pausing. The music was ethereal and not like anything she had ever heard before. The hand at her waist was strong; the hand that held hers was uncommonly gentle. The man's hair was dark. He was taller than her by a foot or more, and his shoulders were broad. The fact that they had never met was oddly unimportant, as was his name. They were moving. Whirling. Dancing.

"Who are you?" She asked after an unknown expanse of time.

"I am Josiah." He answered. "Don't you remember promising me this dance?"

She was confused, but not greatly concerned. "Where are we?"

"Why, we are together!" He said. "I would have thought that was obvious." At this, he had moved her into a twirl and backward into his strong arms – this time, in a full embrace.

"Oh." Was all the reply she felt able to make.

His mouth was at her ear now. What was he saying? Something. But, there was no breath with his words. No breath at all. She tried to focus on what he was saying, but couldn't. The music was fading, too. A sense of profound unease began to fill her.

"Hold on to me! Josiah! They are trying to take me away from this place! They are pulling me away! Josiah! I'm afraid."

"Don't be afraid, my sweet Justine. You will see me again. We are roommates, you and I. Be a brave little sparrow. It is not your time. It is not your time."

Josiah's voice faded away, as did all of the music. She was suddenly aware of a pounding in her head and a searing pain from her arm. The sounds around her were ugly and unfamiliar, but she couldn't open her eyes. As she began to panic – the beeping sound sped up.

Where am I? What has happened to me? Where is Josiah? Why did he leave me here?

Someone came near her and the alarms were silenced. One of her hands was lifted up by the wrist. A woman's voice said, "Justine? Justine? Can you hear me, honey? Try to open your eyes for me? Okay. Maybe not. Can you move your fingers?"

With an effort, Justine tried to remember where her fingers were and how to move them.

"Good! Good girl!" The soothing voice rewarded her. "Justine, do you know where you are?" After a long pause while Justine tried to make her mouth say words, the voice said. "You are at Frederick Memorial Hospital. You have been in an accident."

An accident? A car accident? I don't have a car.

Was I in a cab? Justine's mind worked furiously to remember what had happened to bring her to this place, but nothing would come to her. The pain was out of control. Panic began to take over once more.

"Are you in pain, Justine? Surely you are. Please try to calm down, and I'll see what your doctor has ordered for you. We'll have you feeling much more comfortable soon. Hang on, honey. Stay with us. I'll be right back."

She heard the person – a nurse, she guessed – leave her room. Again, she tried to open her eyes, but they wouldn't cooperate. Her mouth was dry, and her lips were stuck tightly together. She could think words, but was pretty sure she wouldn't be able to speak them. A burst of sharp pain traveled down her arm, and a groan came out of her. Ah. I can make sounds. The pulsing of her heartbeat matched the pounding in her temples, and provided her only measure for the passage of time. Was the pain medication coming? Had she been forgotten and left alone to suffer? Where was. . . ? Where was. . .? She was grasping for the name of someone very dear to her; someone who had kept her safe; someone special. . .but could not find it. This left her feeling inconsolable and even more alone.

Long after Justine had given up hope of being given relief from her suffering, the woman returned. "Justine? Can you hear me? Your doctor has prescribed some medications that will make you feel better."

There was some shuffling and beeping while the woman administered the medication through her IV.

"Okay. Give this a minute or two. I'll be back to check on you in a bit. Try to get some rest."

Justine waited for the blissful absence of pain that had been promised. While she was waiting, she drifted off into a deep sleep.

17 THE SIGN

Outside her café, a good-sized crowd was gathering. It was dinner time on a "Waffle Night," and people were hungry. The sign taped to the door said:

"Café Closed Due to Coma"

"What?" they could be overheard to ask each other. "Coma? That's an odd thing to say, isn't it?" and others said, "Coma? Who?"

It wasn't long before the group of onlookers had doubled in size. The combined impact of the crowd and the sign had been enough to draw passers-by off the sidewalks. Everyone wanted to know what all the excitement was about. Everyone wanted to know about the coma on the sign. Everybody asked everybody else about it, but nobody knew anything.

Opinions were bandied about like ping-pong balls. "Why would anybody put a sign like that up? Coma, or no coma? Does that make sense to you?"

"Well. People might want to know – that's why." A woman in a grey wool coat and red hand-knitted scarf replied, indignantly. "Some of us are regular customers here, and we know Justine."

Now, there was a name. "Justine?" The name was a buzz that was passed overhead from person to person like a balloon at a birthday party. "Justine is in a coma?" They asked.

"I'll bet they took her to Frederick Memorial." The woman in the grey wool coat said with a generous helping of self-importance. "That's the closest one. I'm headed right over there this very minute to see how she's doing! The poor girl."

Other regulars, and even some not-so-regulars, began to think that might be a good idea. The crowd shifted – as one – and made their way to Frederick

Memorial Hospital to check on this Justine person. After all, it was the least they could do. Right?

"Do you think it was a robbery?" Somebody asked as they walked along. "This neighborhood is not what it once was, you know. I remember..."

"No. Nobody would rob that place! There's nothing to take. She mostly feeds homeless folks for free, and never charges much of anything for the rest of us."

"Really? Feeding them for free?"

"Oh, yes. Justine is a rare bird, let me tell you. Give anybody the shirt off her back, she would." (This from a skinny stick of a man, wearing a shirt of questionable origin, and a nearly-new pair of work boots).

Their tales and memories were shared along the route, and it wasn't long before this Justine woman seemed a likely candidate for canonization by the Pope himself. Those that did know her were waxing poetic about her goals and accomplishments, and those that had never heard of her up to this point were solidly convinced that this was someone they very much wanted to know.

It was in this way that Justine awoke that evening to the sounds of a large crowd in the hallway, demanding entrance to her room.

Her eyes opened. Her pain had been greatly lessened. She had lots of questions about what was going on in the hallway. Hell. She had lots of questions, period.

18 CAN I CALL ANYONE?

Justine looked around for a call button, but couldn't find one. Her experience with hospitals was limited to her grandmother's last days in the cancer ward, but she knew what the contraption looked like. After much groping about, she located a thick grey cord that had been draped over one of the bed railings and started to reel it in.

Aha! Got you!

With relief, she pressed the button and waited.

The commotion was still going on at full volume in the hallway outside her door. There were so many voices, that Justine couldn't make out what anybody was saying. They wanted to see somebody? Had she "been robbed?" -- Something along those lines.

Must be somebody famous on the ward. She thought. *Great. I'll probably wither and die in here.*

Justine pushed the call button again. She waited -- again. Nothing.

It was just about then that her thirst took over. There was a sweating pitcher of ice water on the tray next to her bed with a large, white cup sitting next to it; both were just out of reach. Her left arm was a science experiment; suspended from a sturdy assembly of shiny chrome and pulley contraptions. She winced. Ouch. When her pain meds wore off, that was going to hurt.

Justine became intensely aware of two things at the same time; her nose itched, and she needed to go to the bathroom. Where was the nursing staff? She pushed the call button three times in rapid succession with no response before resorting to the tried-and-true, low-tech method.

"NURSE!! HELLO?! I NEED SOME HELP IN HERE! NURSE? ANYBODY?"

Her outburst was followed by an awed silence in the hallway. This lasted for only a fraction of a second, before she heard a vaguely familiar female voice booming, "That's her! Get Outta' my way!"

Before Justine knew what was happening, her bed was surrounded by a crowd of café regulars and perfect strangers. Between the pain meds and her urgent need to access a toilet, bed pan or diaper, she was too overwhelmed to make much sense of the invasion.

Martha Koch took charge, immediately.

"You poor thing!" She exclaimed. "What can we do for you? Are you thirsty?"

"Oh, yes." Justine answered gratefully. "I've been pushing this call button for what seems like hours, and . . ."

Martha poured a generous amount of water into the cup, inserted a bendable straw and held it to her mouth.

The first sip acted like solvent to separate her

parched tongue from the roof of her mouth. It was better than anything she had ever tasted; cold and clear. Justine sucked hungrily at the straw, and was not pleased when Martha pulled the cup away too soon.

"Not too much, honey." She warned. "Nothing like a flood of cold liquid to make a patient lose her lunch."

Justine nodded.

Everyone began to talk at once. They wanted to know about the robbery, a coma, a sign on the café door?

Martha's large, gravelly, voice boomed above the cacophony.

"Quiet! Can't you see the poor thing is overwhelmed? Everybody out! This minute! If you wait patiently, in the lobby, I'll be along to answer all of your questions. Right now, Justine needs care and privacy!"

As the last person filed out and the room fell silent, Justine's gratitude knew no bounds.

"God bless you, Martha. What the hell is going on around here? Who were those people? Why am I in here?"

"There will be plenty of time for all of that, later. Are you comfortable? Do you need anything?"

"Honestly? I need to go to the bathroom. Is there a bed pan around here, anywhere? I'm about to mess the sheets."

Martha examined the I.V. set-up and the suspension gadget, carefully. "I think we can do better than that." She said. "Don't worry, Darlin'. Before I was a useless old busybody, I was a nurse for 35 years."

Justine's arm was gently lifted out of the sling apparatus and the I.V. pole was wheeled competently alongside as she was guided into the bathroom. Sitting on the toilet was a relief, and she'd made it just in time. Her need had been so great that having Martha on standby had been no cause for embarrassment.

"Need help, Luv?"

"Nope. I've got this. May need a lift back to the

bed, though."

"I'm here, and here I'll stay." She replied, with a mother's firm resolve.

My mother! Justine thought, frantically. *Has anybody called my mother?*

Martha had her back in the bed, snug as five puppies in a basket, in no time. Justine let out a heavy sigh.

"Better?"

"Oh, yes. You are an angel, Martha." She smiled, weakly.

"Does your family know you're in here?" She asked. "Do you need me to call anybody?"

"My mom. She's all the family I have. But, no. I don't want to call her until I know more about what happened and how long they are planning to keep me. Mom isn't in the best of health. I hate to worry her over nothing."

"Are you sure? I'm a mother, and I like to worry

over nothing. That's what we do best."

"Where are your nurses?" She asked, with her hands on her generous hips. "A good nurse would have been in here to check on you three times by now."

"I don't know. I saw one at some point. . ."

"Well, that's going to change – right now!" Martha turned on her heel and stormed out of the room, ignoring Justine's weak protests to the contrary.

As much as Justine hated to make a fuss, she had to admit she was grateful to have somebody like Martha in her corner. Funny, she had never considered Mrs. Koch a close friend – more of a "regular" at the café. And, who were all those people? She had recognized Sticks, and Jenny Bryant; that heavy kid and his brother. . . What were their names? She put her good hand to her temple and rubbed. Her head was beginning to throb again.

19 THE SENTINEL

Josiah was furious with William (known throughout the granary as "Dangling Will") for his vulgar display of ill temper. "What was all that fuss about? Just look at what you've done, you silly ass!" They looked at Justine's crumpled body as it lay there at the base of the stairs. She was unconscious and barely breathing; her glorious hair fanned out around her like a benediction.

"I do hope she'll be alright." Will said, with the appropriate amount of regret in his voice.   "I've assured her discovery, at any rate. Help is coming."

"It was the very least you could do." Josiah scolded. "And, what of the roof? How shall she put that right? You know full well that she can't afford a repair like this."

"I was angry." He put a hand to his forehead. "There was a living girl . . . she . . ."

"Don't put yourself out trying to excuse this mess, William." Josiah folded his arms and considered Will for a space of time. "If you were still breathing, I'd be tempted to strangle you."

"But, she was the messenger, Josiah! She arrived in a white carriage – just as foretold. I was standing at my window – looking down at her – and, as God is my witness, she raised her eyes to meet mine. She saw me, Josiah! But, though I waited patiently for her to come, she did not." His grief was plain to see. "The last I saw of her she was riding away through the snow."

"Justine? Are you up there?" A concerned voice called out from the second floor.

Both spirits faded away just in time for the queer little shopkeeper to stumble onto the landing.

"Justine!! Oh my God!"

Now, standing in a dark corner of her hospital room, Josiah reached out to sweep a strand of hair from Justine's eyes. In her sleep, Justine smiled. He felt a momentary stab of guilt for wishing she had not survived the fall, but then brushed it aside. After all, a man could do much worse than to spend an eternity at her side . . .

His mind shifted, instead, to Dangling Will's story. He knew that some of the living had been blessed with a gift for second sight. Had such a one come to the granary? And, in a chariot? Certainly not. In the bed, Justine shifted slightly and groaned. He moved forward to look on her more closely.

How had this woman become so dear to him? He told himself that his feelings were those of gratitude for her protection and preservation of the granary, but was that true? Watching her dance with an imaginary partner, night after night, had been so enchanting and poignant. How could such a fine, graceful and giving woman be so alone? A sound from the hallway caused Josiah to melt back into the shadows.

A nurse entered the room, quietly switched on the bathroom light -- so as not to startle the room's occupants -- then obtained Justine's temperature, blood pressure, and pulse rate under the watchful eye of Mrs. Koch.

Josiah watched the proceedings with interest. Things had certainly changed over the last century. Everything beeped and lit up in such an impressive way. At any rate, they seemed to know what they were about in this hospital, and the Lass was doing well, so Josiah returned to the granary and his responsibilities there.

His first task would be to gather more information about this "Messenger," and her "Chariot."

20 FLOWERS FROM FENTIS

The days came and went without much to distinguish one from the next. Justine's eyes often came to rest on the enormous bouquet of roses that now dominated her nightstand. They were impossible to ignore. She couldn't imagine how many roses were in the arrangement, but there seemed to be one to represent every color of the rainbow.

They were truly lovely; everyone said so. But, it was proving impossible to get in and out of bed without causing the tall vase to totter dangerously towards one side or the other. She was tempted to donate them to the nurse's station, or just throw them away, but Arthur might show up at any time and she didn't want to seem ungrateful . . .

His visits had been awkward. When a man shows up at the hospital with a bouquet like that – assumptions are made. Even Martha left the room, discreetly, when Arthur had shown up at the door – a wall of flowers with a pair of legs.

"Oh, Martha! Come back! You don't have to leave!" She had called out with some degree of desperation. But all she had gotten was a conspiratorial wink in response.

"Hello, Lovely Lady!" He had oozed with familiarity, setting the bouquet on the only available surface. "You look a lot better than you did the last time I saw you!"

Justine smiled weakly. "Oh. Hi, Arthur. How's the shop?"

"Oh, business is booming. You know. I can barely keep enough merchandise on the floor these days!"

Right. She thought, trying hard not to roll her

eyes. *You haven't made a sale since you opened your doors. Makes no difference to me. Just pay your rent – on time – every month.*

He had pulled up a chair and launched himself into the heroic blow-by-blow description of how he had "saved her life." How (according to Arthur) he had heard a loud crash and had demanded that his customers leave the store so that he could run to determine its cause. Blah, blah, blah, so on and so forth. But, when he had reached for her hand at the climactic moment, Justine had jerked it away as though she had discovered a sudden need to scratch an itchy place on her bad arm.

"Are you ever going to tell me how you ended up in that terrible state? Do you remember anything about the accident?"

Justine had been asked this question a million times. She had no recollection of any events leading up to her fall. She had even been surprised to learn of the caved in roof beam. It made sense that the two were somehow related, but she could only assume that she had heard the collapse, gone to investigate, and in her hurry to get the repairs underway had lost her footing on the stairs.

"I don't remember anything, Arthur. Nothing at all."

"Well, that darn striped cat was wandering around up there when I discovered you. I've warned you that those cats are not safe! It must have wound between your feet and tripped you up. Besides, they really do stink up the place, Justine. You should call the SPCA and have them removed."

Tiger Boy? Was that how it happened? He does get underfoot sometimes. She bit her lip.

"I couldn't do that! They are my family. Haven't you ever had a pet?" She was now impatient for the little bougar to leave. "Especially Tiger Boy; my goodness. . . he's been with me for years."

"Well, worry not. Selma has been running the Café in your absence, and she wanted you to know that the dirty little things are well cared for."

He must have seen the irritation growing in her

face, because he changed tack, immediately.

"Do you like the roses? I went all over town to find a florist who could do this for me. Some women get red, and some get white, but a woman such as you should receive every color there is!"

Smarmy bastard sure is proud of himself. Dream on, Mergatroid.

"They are very nice." She managed. "Certainly brighten up the room."

As Arthur beamed and reached for her hand again, Justine faked a yawn and stretch. "Arthur, I am very tired. The pain medication makes me sleepy, as you can imagine. . ."

"Go ahead and rest, my dear! I will watch over you while you sleep."

Gack.

"No, Arthur, honestly. I'd rest much better on my own. Okay?"

The pause that followed was intensely

uncomfortable. He was trying to lock eyes with her in a meaningful way, and she was running out of other things to look at.

"Okay, Dearest. Whatever you say! Don't worry about anything, though. Okay? I am supervising everything that goes on in that building, and there will be no shenanigans on my watch." Finally, he stood. Justine sighed with relief, while at the same time feeling very sorry for Selma. She would have to remember to call the café to give moral support.

"Oh! Look! Your husband has brought you such beautiful flowers!" A nurse had walked in just then and squealed with obvious delight – somehow managing to prolong Justine's misery. Arthur beamed and pulled himself up to his full height.

"Thank you. He's not my husband. We are just business associates."

Needless to say, her attempt at clarification was not well received by Mr. Fentis.

"Ah. Well. I wish I had a business associate like

that!" Said the nurse, with a knowing wink in Arthur's direction.

Justine dropped her head into her only available hand. *Double gack.*

21 AN ALTERATION IN PLANS

Kathy Harold was getting anxious about her wedding dress. The woman had promised to call in only a few days, and more than two weeks had passed with no word. She wasn't the type to nag or hurry anyone along, but she knew something would have to be done soon, and that she was probably going to have to be the one to do it.

Chewing on her lower lip, Kathy dialed the number on the woman's business card. She was going to hang up after the third ring, but somebody picked up.

"Hello? This is Justine."

"Hello, Mrs. Fournier! This is Kathy Harold. I. . ."

"Oh! Kathy! Yes. I remember you, of course. And, call me "Justine" please. There's no need for last names."

Kathy could hear the smile in her voice, and the image of Justine's face came clearly to mind.

"Kathy," Justine kept talking, "You have no way of knowing this, but I've had a terrible fall and have been in the hospital for . . ." She paused, as if to count the days.

"Oh! I'm so sorry to hear that! Are you going to be okay?"

"Yes. Thank you. I will be back at the shop by next Monday."

"Well, that explains why I haven't heard anything about the dress. I was getting concerned."

"That's what I need to tell you. Your alterations are finished! And, I was so looking forward to being there when you picked up your dress. . ."

"Me too! Actually, I was kind-of hoping that you wouldn't mind if I brought my fiancée, Billy, along? We are both . . . you know . . . able to see and hear things . . ." Kathy gulped, feeling suddenly vulnerable. Did Justine even recall their conversation about the paranormal activity at the granary?

"That would be fantastic! But, you don't have to wait until next Monday to pick up your dress. I will arrange for you to have the run of the whole building – let's say Saturday night? I will make sure that my assistant is there to let you in, and that your dress is hanging on the rack by the door. Would that be okay?"

Kathy was tingling from head to toe. They could wander around the place alone? At night? They had plans for dinner with some friends on Saturday, but Kathy was subconsciously cancelling without hesitation.

"Wow! Really? That would be so great!" She could hear Justine's laughter on the other end, and it was contagious.

"Try not to be so disappointed!" Justine joked.

"Oh. No. It would be great with you there, too. But . . ."

"I know. This will be more of an adventure, right?"

Kathy returned her laughter and conceded the point. "Right."

"Okay. Then it's a date! I always hide the key under the second tire in the stack of old tires behind the building. Can you remember that?"

"Sure!"

"And I'll let everybody know that you will be watching the place for me Saturday night, so that there will be no confusion about why you're there."

"Oh! Thank you, Mrs. Fournier . . . Justine, I mean. I am so excited!"

Kathy could hear voices in the background.

"Okay. They're here to poke and prod me, unmercifully, so I'll have to sign off."

"Okay. Hope you feel better! And, thanks!"

Kathy pushed "End" on her cell and sat down. She had to call Bill right away! But, he was at work, and that wasn't okay. As a memory crutch, she scrolled through her contact list looking for someone to call. Nobody. Well, nobody who would understand, anyway.

She'd have to wait until Billy got home around 6:00 p.m. to call.

With a heavy sigh, she decided to spend the time doing some research on the building's history. *Knowledge is power.* She thought as she mounted the steps to her room. *And, I'm not sure why, but I think I'm going to need all the power I can get.*

22 RETURN OF THE MESSENGER

The roads looked very different at night, as did the granary when they arrived.

"Is this it?" Bill had asked, craning his head up to take in the full scope of the old building. "It's huge!"

"I know. It looks kind of intimidating from here." She gulped, nervously.

"Drive through there to the back." Billy pointed to a small driveway on their left.

"Yeah. Okay."

They had both been surprised by how far back the building went. But, it wasn't long before the van's headlights skimmed over the stack of old tires Justine had told them to look for.

"There they are!" Kathy said. "I'll park while you jump out and find the key."

Their eyes met and the shared trepidation and anticipation caused a bout of nervous laughter. Billy leaned towards her for a brief kiss before jumping out of the car in search of the key. By the time Kathy had parked the van and shut down the headlights, Billy was walking towards her with something in his hand.

"Got it!" They laughed again, and looked around nervously.

"What happens if the police catch us going inside?"

"I think we'll be okay. But we should hurry, don't you think?"

"Somebody is sure to notice our flashlights and stuff."

They looked at each other and said,

simultaneously, "Flashlights!!" which caused another burst of laughter.

Kathy ran back to the van and opened up the back. They had brought a couple of cases full of paranormal investigation equipment along, as well as a cooler with snacks and sodas for later. Bill met her at the tailgate and took one of the cases and the cooler.

Now, with all of the equipment and the key in hand, they could put off their adventure no longer. The young couple approached the door together only to stop abruptly.

"Is this the key to the front door, the back door, or one of those side doors?" He asked.

"She never said!" Kathy wondered why they were both whispering. "Let's just try them all."

"Great." He looked right and left. "Jeez. I sure hope there're not any cops or homeless people or muggers around. . ."

The key fit the glassed-in door that served as the café entrance in the front – or the last one they tried -- as luck would have it. The lock was tricky, and the light switches were not as handy as they might have been, but once they were locked inside, the couple began to relax.

"There's my dress!" Kathy touched the dress bag on the rack. "Remember. No peeking!"

"I don't need to see that dress to know you're going to be gorgeous in it." He slipped his arms around her waist from behind and pulled her close.

"This place is haunted, isn't it." This was a statement – not a question.

"Yep." He kissed her hair. "I can smell the history."

They both breathed deeply to more fully experience the sense of age in the air. It smelled of dust and stones and thick wooden beams. The silence was broken only by the ticking of an outdated clock/radio on the Café's kitchen counter.

"I bet they'll be happy to have someone to talk to." He said. "We might even be able to point somebody in the right direction while we're here."

"Okay, handsome. She took his hands in hers and freed herself from the embrace. "Let's get this show on the road!"

The cases were laid open on one of the tables and each item of equipment was loaded with fresh batteries and slipped into the vests Kathy had purchased in the hunting department of the Bass Pro Shop. They pulled on matching baseball caps with lights clipped on their bills and switched them on. When most of the vest pockets had been utilized, they grabbed their digital recorders and hit "record" at the same time. Billy nodded to Kathy, and she spoke.

"This is Bill Fische and Kathy Harold. Tonight we are investigating the Old Granary in Frederick, Maryland." She added the address, the date and the time, and they followed the beams of their lights towards a shadowy stairwell that was located in the rear of the Café.

"Hello, Ghosties!" Kathy called out, eerily. "We're coming to see you!" The young couple laughed again, in unison.

The building had been strangely free of any echo, but they both knew that her words had been heard.

23 NOT ONE, BUT TWO

Pacing in front of the window, "Dangling Will" Poston waited for the messengers to reach him. He had been thrilled to see the familiar white chariot cruising slowly by, but his excitement had turned to anxiety when it had driven through the side lot without stopping.

Where are you going? Why do you not stop and talk with me? He felt his anger mounting, but remembered Josiah's warning against future outbursts and began to pace back and forth, instead.

As each door had been rattled, in turn, his hopes had begun to rise. Unlike the other ghosts inhabiting the granary, Will was unable to move freely about the building, or he would have gone downstairs to greet them. He had always assumed that this restriction had been imposed due to the fact that he had caused his own death. As it had been a much more lenient consequence than the fiery hell he had been taught to expect during his lifetime, he had been quick to accept it.

Josiah had the most freedom to move about. He had stayed in the granary by choice, having been given the option of moving on into the glaring light that appeared by him every morning. For him, the building had been a happy place where he had been able to pile up one success after another. Dangling Will would have preferred to move on. He wanted more than anything to be reunited with his son . . . Surely, the boy would be waiting anxiously for him on the other side? He wrung his ghostly hands and resumed his pacing.

It was with great relief that he heard the front door creaking open, and he listened carefully for the sound of the messenger. What he heard after that came as quite a surprise.

Two? Two of them? Young, by the sound of them; male and female. Why has Josiah gone away for so long? What should I do? There is no point in trying to hide, as the female has already seen me and knows that I am waiting for her."

Will's excitement began to escalate, causing him to flicker between a glowing orb and a full-body manifestation. He tried, compulsively, to clear his throat before realizing that he no longer had one.

They are coming! They are asking the spirits to answer questions, but Josiah isn't here, and the others are, most-likely, to be found in the cellar.

The Indian Shaman and the young boys he had sacrificed at the mouth of the "Great Hole in the Earth," had ventured upwards through the granary only once. William had been fascinated by the bright colors of their face paint and their comparative nakedness. Though the language of the dead was universal, no words had been exchanged. In fact, the natives seemed to be as curious about his appearance as he had been of theirs.

The men and women who had perished in the

fire of 1870 had been so near the exit as to be heard by the townsfolk assembled outside, but their way was sealed off, and they soon succumbed to the hungry flames and the smoke of tons upon tons of burning grain. Josiah believed that these spirits inhabited the cellar because it stayed cool and dark, but nobody really knew for sure, and Will had never laid eyes on them.

Dangling Will Poston's reverie came to an abrupt halt and his eyes snapped to the staircase that opened onto the fourth floor. Strange lights moved in the stairwell, and he could hear the footsteps of the living approaching. He bowed his head to make one last, urgent, appeal for forgiveness and freedom from his earthly confinement.

24 RELEASED AT LAST

Earlier that same evening, Justine was sitting up in the chair by her bed. She had just finished dinner when Doctor Bauer showed up for his evening rounds.

He was very tall and thin with sandy hair. She guessed his age at 50, or so. His eyes were a slate blue/gray, and he was one of those people who always looked like he must be up to something. There was a certain twinkle in his eyes, and his cheeks could dimple when he grinned.

"Well! Look who's feeling better!" He exclaimed, smiling.

"Hello, Doctor. Yes. Thank you."

He bent his head to flip through her charts. A cloud came over his face for a moment, and she just had to ask.

"Is something wrong?"

"No. Nothing serious. I'm just not happy with your blood work up."

"Why? What's wrong with my blood?"

Dr. Bauer seemed to shrug his worry away as he closed the charts. "Your white cell counts are a bit high. Nothing out of normal ranges, but I'd feel better if you followed up with your family doctor in a few weeks, just to be safe."

"Does that mean I'm getting out of here?" She asked with hope radiating from her face.

"The head injury was our main cause for concern, as you know. Brain swelling and fever can be deadly if they aren't addressed immediately."

Justine nodded. The nurses had been telling her that the head injury had stabilized.

"As for your arm. . ." He flipped another couple of sheets on the clipboard. "The surgery was largely successful. You will have two titanium rods between the shoulder and the elbow of your left arm for the rest of your life. We are setting up a series of appointments with a Physical Therapist to help you regain a more natural range of motion."

"Will I set off the metal detectors at the airport?" She asked, only half-serious.

"People always ask me that!" He dropped both arms to his sides. "You might. Some machines are more sensitive than others. I will give you a card to carry in your wallet that explains the rods in your left arm. But, the rods are relatively small as compared to a hip or knee replacement, so you'll probably slip right through security."

She brushed her hair back with her good hand. "That's okay. I never go anywhere anyway."

"You will be going home, though, young lady! Stay the remainder of the weekend. Get as much rest as you can. We will discharge you on Monday."

"Yay!" She raised her hand.

"Will there be anybody to assist you at home?"

Justine thought about lying. She really thought she'd be fine on her own, and couldn't wait to be back home again.

"Yes. That's no problem. I'll have some friends stay over for a few days."

"Okay, then. I'll be back Monday morning to sign your discharge papers. Plan to have somebody here for you around noon. Go to your physical therapy appointments, without fail! They will make a profound difference in the success or failure of your recovery!" He warned in a fatherly tone. "I'll expect to see you in three weeks for a follow-up. You might want to call and schedule that on Monday. Be sure to tell Rhonda that this is a post-op follow-up."

"Thanks, Dr. Bauer. I will."

From his place in the shadows, Josiah was smiling from ear-to-ear. It would be good to have things back to normal again. He wondered who was going to pick her up on Monday, and hoped that she didn't call the bizarre little man with the slicked-back hair.

25 GHOST ADVENTURES

Bill and Kathy switched on the lights when they reached the second floor landing. They had agreed that they'd only go "Lights Out" once they had gotten a feel for their surroundings. The building was very old, and they knew it could be hiding potential hazards. Once on, the lights revealed a short reception area that opened onto a large room (Bill estimated that it was at least 25'x 25') that was dissected by huge wooden beams. The whole back wall was filled with windows – framed in the same dark wood as the floors and columns. The glass was bowed and bubbled and ancient. The lights that shone in from outside were charmingly warped. Along one wall there were old church pews and assorted folding chairs; along the opposite wall were some scattered round tables and a couple of derelict sofas.

"Oh, Jeez!" Kathy made a face. The odor of cat urine and feces was overpowering. "Think she has a few dozen cats?"

"I'd say at least that many." He grimaced. "What's in here?"

Together they ventured into a small opening to their right. It wasn't easy, as the area had been piled high with trash, furniture and discarded clothing. Just a few feet into the chaos they discovered a tiny bathroom. It was surprisingly clean, with a small selection of toiletries on a shelf by the sink.

"This must be the one Justine uses." Kathy observed. "I guess her room must be around here, somewhere."

"Ugh! How can she stand the stench?" He coughed in the dust and fumes.

"She's been in the hospital for a while, too, you know? I wonder who's been watching the cats for her?"

"Ah. You have a point, there."

"Bill, would you mind poking around in the café to see if you can find some garbage bags or bags of fresh kitty litter? She's put boxes around for them to use, but they're all full to the point of overflowing."

"Only you would think about cleaning up somebody else's cat crap." He grinned.

She put one hand on her hip and leaned her head to one side just a bit. "That's why you love me, though, right, William James Fische?"

Bill laughed and headed off in the direction of the stairway. "Don't get into any trouble while I'm gone."

As he disappeared around the corner, Kathy continued to investigate the piles of refuse in search of an opening. Not five feet away from the bathroom, she discovered what she had been looking for -- a narrow gap through which she could easily squeeze.

Once through, she found herself in a large, open space. The LED lights that lined the bill of her ball cap fell upon a table lamp, which she clicked on without hesitation.

"Where are you?" Billy was calling from the large room nearby. "Kathy?"

"I'm in here!" She called. "Wait just a second. I'm coming out. You have got to see this!"

Billy seemed surprised to see her emerging from the teetering wall of trash. "Something back in there?" He asked, scratching his head.

"Yep." She saw the box of garbage bags in his hand and cheered. "Yay! No luck with the kitty litter?"

"Nope. And, I looked all around. She probably keeps that up here, don't you think? I mean, who keeps their kitty litter in a restaurant?"

"You have a point." Kathy conceded. "Let's just keep our eyes open for it. I'd hate to come home from the hospital to this mess, wouldn't you?"

"So, what was back in there?" Billy asked,

suddenly curious.

"Oh! It's pretty wild! Follow me."

Kathy took Billy's hand and pulled him through the maze to what had to be Justine's bedroom.

"Wow. . ." Billy stood in the opening, taking everything in. "Is that her?" He asked, appreciatively.

"Yes. I told you she was beautiful." Kathy answered, with awe.

The walls of this room were literally covered with portraits of Justine. Every medium you could think of had been represented in the display; pastels, oils, watercolors, charcoal, pencil, and pen. Justine had been depicted in various stages of undress, standing, sitting or lying down. Regardless of the style or size of the portraits, they were all amazing works of art.

The couple stood there for several long minutes.

"Wow."

"You already said that." Kathy whispered.

26 PATIENCE IS A VIRTUE

Voices drifted up to him from the second floor. William Poston wanted to confront the messengers with all of his heart, but had been forbidden to move from this cursed arena of his untimely death! He couldn't imagine what they were doing down there, when he was up here. Saving his energy, Will remained invisible, but his restless spirit continued to pace anxiously back and forth in front of the window.

What if they leave? Would they do that? His thoughts kept returning to the heartbreak he had felt the last time; when the girl had left. . .

They mustn't leave again! I couldn't bear it. I simply couldn't! Surely they have come to speak to me?

Josiah is not here, so. . .

His thoughts prodded his fear like a tongue worries a loose tooth. All attempts at remaining calm and patient were trampled by the simple fact that the messenger had seen him before, and yet had left without speaking to him.

Yes. But, now she has come back with another messenger. She has come back to see me. Maybe she didn't know how to help me, and he does? Maybe she was afraid to confront me on her own?

Even as the last thought formed in his mind, he dismissed it. The messenger's eyes had shown no fear; curiosity perhaps; acceptance. . .

Was this hell, then? Like the victim of a shipwreck floating in shark-infested for so many years, only to be shunned and ignored by the only people who owned a boat?

Stay calm. Stay calm. He repeated. *They have much to see in this place. There are many chambers and the living must walk to move between them.*

Will was tempted to cause a ruckus, as he had done before to draw help for the injured woman. But, what if that frightened the messengers away? No. He must wait. It wouldn't be that much longer, now. The messengers were on their way. The nightmare would be over soon, and he could be reunited with his son.

He tried to conjure up an image of James' face and couldn't. As much as he treasured their short time together among the living, his memories had faded to mist long ago. It was his overwhelming grief that never left him. The knowledge that his son had died a horrible death that could have been so simply averted. Why had he insisted that James work on the fourth floor that day? Why hadn't he been there to pull his son back from the edge of the gaping maw that was the silo? Every man there had been quick to tell him he was not at fault. "It was God's will." Or "It was his time."

The guilt and grief had torn William apart over the following days and weeks. His thoughts had been full of dark things and evil portents. The house that they had shared was cloaked in a heavy stillness where the ticking of the mantel clock had filled his ears with the message that his son was dead and he was living. What right had he to live and breathe, when he had failed to save his son?

To this very instant, he would swear that it was the ticking of that malevolent clock that had seduced him to hunt out a sturdy rope.

Once the wicked plan had formed in his mind, it had played out again and again during both his waking and sleeping hours until that final act had seemed the only plausible way to atone for his son's death and join him in whatever journey awaited them.

William Poston had walked into the granary in the early hours of a Saturday morning; had climbed the stairs with a rope and a heavy heart; and had ended his time among the living.

But, he had crossed over only to find himself alone and unable to move more than a few yards from where his body still hung from a sturdy wooden rafter. His constant plea since that moment had been for mercy. Surely God would show compassion for a man who had only sought to end his unbearable suffering?

It was from these sad reflections that Dangling Will looked up to see the lights and hear the sounds of their approach. He gathered up all of the surrounding energy in preparation for his upcoming manifestation.

27 GETTING DOWN TO BUSINESS

The couple had found a huge, unopened, bag of kitty litter on the landing of the third floor, so – to Billy's poorly-veiled frustration – they busied themselves with the task of emptying and filling the cat boxes that had been positioned in various places on both the second and third floors.

Completing that set of tasks left them both sorely in need of a garbage bin and a wash-up. Billy grumbled all the way down to the café, but he was still gentleman enough to lug the heavy bag full of repugnant feline leavings and take them around back to the garbage bin. Smiling, Kathy held the door for him and made sure it shut tightly behind him once he had returned to her.

"That will go down in history as the most ridiculous, unnecessary and unpleasant wastes of time. . ." He paused, mid-grouch, to gauge Kathy's expression. Getting her angry was not something he wanted to risk over cat poop.

"C'mon, Honey. Would you want to drag yourself home from the hospital to ten overflowing litter boxes?"

"I don't have to worry about that, as I never intend to own a cat."

Bill was generously lathering his hands, wrists and forearms with a bar of Ivory soap that he'd found in the café's bathroom when he became aware of the fact that Kathy had not budged from her position by the back door.

When he found her, she was standing resolutely with her arms crossed and a look of indignation on her sweet round face.

"What?" He asked, with a faint-hearted

courage he didn't feel.

"And where do you think Midnight is going to live after we get married? Hmm?"

He gulped. "Oh."

"Did you think I was going to leave him with my mom?"

"Um."

"That cat has been one of my dearest and closest companions for over ten years, Billy Fische. I've known him longer than I've known you!"

He moved forward with his mouth curved into a tentative grin. "Okay. I forgot about Midnight. I'm sorry. I guess I was just feeling sorry for myself about having to clean up that stinky mess."

Kathy uncrossed her arms and allowed him to slip his arms around her waist. He kissed her neck in that tickly way of his, and they shared a laugh.

"That was a very kind and thoughtful thing for you to do. Really. It was."

"Of course it was!" She took long strides towards the bathroom sink. "And, now that you've helped me to do it – you'll have good Karma for weeks!"

Billy ripped a couple of paper towels off the roll and handed them to Kathy with a smile. They shared a chaste kiss and looked into each other's eyes with exaggerated longing.

"Can we get back to the business at hand, here?"

"Let's do it!" She replied, and they raced each other up the stairs to the fourth floor.

28 FACE TO FACE WITH DANGLING WILL

By the time they had reached the third floor landing, the young couple was feeling a bit winded. They probably told themselves that the slower pace they had adopted while climbing the next set of stairs was the result of physical exhaustion, but, as they approached the top of the building, the pair began to feel a difference in the atmosphere. They exchanged glances.

"He's up here."

"I know. I can feel him."

"He is very sad, isn't he?"

"Yes. That's what I saw in his eyes that day. So much sadness."

"Is he the spirit of the boy who fell into the silo from up here?"

"I don't think so. He appeared to be much older. I think he is the man who . . ."

"Oh." Bill didn't need her to finish that sentence. They had studied the building's history prior to getting there, and both of them knew who this would be and why he was still here. If you were able to see him in the window from the street below, maybe he will show himself to us tonight.

"Maybe." She replied. "But, I don't know if he will feel secure enough with both of us here; especially with us standing right here."

"Hello?" Kathy checked her digital recorder to make sure it was on and recording. "William Poston?" Sliding the recorder into a pocket in her vest, she then removed her K2 meter and switched it on.

"Mr. Poston?" Bill tried. "We know you are

here, and we want to help you – if we can. Please don't be afraid to show yourself to us? My name is William, too. Um. I go by 'Bill'. This is Kathy."

The eerie silence stretched outwards to blanket them in a poignant anticipation. They felt the spirit's overwhelming sadness.

Kathy spoke up. "Will? Where did you hang yourself in this room? Can you make a sound? Can you knock on a wall or a window to let us know where you are?"

The couple stood absolutely still and listened for his signal.

Tap. Tap. Tap.

"It came from the far end. Back there."

Kathy followed Bill through the dense shadows for several feet before both of them came to an abrupt halt.

"Whoa."

"I wonder what happened here?" Kathy said,

looking up and seeing the night sky through a massive hole in the roof. "Do you think this is where he died?"

Tap. Tap. Tap.

This time the sound was clear enough to make Kathy jump – in spite of herself.

"That was tapping on a window pane."

"Yes. I think you're right."

"Mr. Poston? Is that you, sir? We heard about your son's tragic fall into the silo. Is that why you decided to end your life?"

"Take a few photos in here." Kathy instructed. "My K2 is picking up something."

The camera flashed and whirred several times with Billy pausing every now and then to review the photos he had taken for any signs of paranormal activity.

Kathy walked towards the window to the right of the caved in timber and stopped when the K2 meter began to beep in a frantic rhythm.

"Mr. Poston? Is that you, sir?" When the beeping stopped, Kathy spoke up again. "Okay. We found you. Thanks for the tapping. It worked great." She raised the K2 meter up to show it around. "This is a machine that shows electro-magnetic activity, Mr. Poston. We can use it to have a conversation with you. Try standing off to my side and waving one hand in front of it. Can you try that for me? Don't worry, it can't hurt you."

After a brief pause the meter beeped once.

The couple exchanged glances again and grinned.

"Okay! That is all you need to do. I will ask questions, and you can answer "Yes" or "No," by causing the meter to beep once for "Yes" and twice for "No." Do you understand?"

Again, the meter beeped once.

"That's perfect. Thank you." Kathy took a deep breath and asked her first question.

29 K2 SESSION

For over 30 minutes their questions were answered with a firm "Yes" or "No." Soon after that, however, Kathy and Bill lost all contact with Mr. Poston. They knew that these sessions could be exhausting for spirits. Besides, they had already learned everything they needed to know about why Mr. Poston's spirit had never left the granary.

The digital recorder had caught the entire "conversation," and they were going to have to review every second of that recording for any evidence of William's voice – should he have said anything during the K2 session.

"Mr. Poston? We are going to leave you alone

now. You must be very tired. We will be back in a few days, though. Okay?"

"Thank you for putting up with all of our questions. We hope to talk to you again soon." Billy added.

The couple left the fourth floor feeling pretty exhausted themselves. According to answers from Mr. Poston, there were still quite a few spirits in the granary for them to talk to, and they were excited to venture into the mysteries of the ground floor and cellar. But, first, they planned on a break in the café to eat some of the snacks they had brought along. They had only been investigating for 3 hours, but those last few minutes had been pretty intense.

It was hard to spend much time wandering around in that building without feeling dirty. They reached the ground floor within seconds of each other and made their way to the bathroom to wash their hands and splash their faces with warm water.

"Oreos?" Billy asked. "Diet Coke?"

"Yes. Thanks. That sounds just right."

"Want to play back the K2 session while we eat?"

"No. I'd rather wait until we have headphones on and can really devote our full attention to it."

He nodded, fighting gallantly with the crinkly clear plastic that was keeping the both of them from their well-deserved Oreos. "Yeah. I'll bet you anything that he was talking to us the whole time; not just passing his hand in front of the meter." The wrapping finally tore open – a bit too violently – and a cookie flew out to break into pieces on the floor.

"What a waste!" Kathy mourned, dramatically. "Next time, I'm going to open the package."

They laughed and grabbed a small stack of cookies each. It was warmer in the café. On the upper floors, there were windows with no glass in them that had been taped up with trash bags to keep out the wind. As they had progressed through the building, it had become apparent that the wind was winning that battle. Many of the garbage bags had been flapping noisily with their tape rendered useless. Justine had warned them to dress for this, however, so they had been prepared.

Still, as the night had worn on, the combined factors of the dust, the overwhelming musk of cat urine and feces, the freezing gusts of night air, and the need for constant vigilance in navigating the unique terrain of the granary in comparative darkness, had left them somewhat drained.

Billy yawned. "What time is it, anyway?"

Kathy dug into her vest pocket for her cell and lit the screen. "Early. Only a few minutes after midnight."

"Oh, Jeez." He stuffed another cookie into his mouth and chewed appreciatively. "I'm ready to call it a night, aren't you?"

"We can't do that!" She sat up straighter. "We haven't even done this floor!"

"Oh, criminy, Kathy. I'm beat."

"Me too." She confessed. "Why don't we compromise and just do a quick sweep through these last two floors? I'll keep an eye on the meter, keep the recorder running; and, you just flash a ton of pictures in every room. We should be able to finish up in another hour and then we can pack up and head home. What do you say?"

"Sounds good to me." He stretched and began to pack up the food.

Kathy dampened a paper towel in the Café's kitchen and wiped up the demolished cookie fragments.

"How are the batteries?" Kathy asked.

Billy checked the camera and both K2 meters and found that the camera's battery had been drained down to almost nothing over the time they had been upstairs. "Wow. Mr. Poston must have been drawing power from these." He said, as he found a set of fresh batteries and made the replacement.

"That was a long session for us, so you know it must have been difficult for him."

"Apparently."

"Okay. Are we all set?"

"I'm ready whenever you are." He quipped.

30 WHEN THEY SPEAK

The very next afternoon, the young couple sat across from each other at the kitchen table in Kathy's house reviewing evidence. For the uninitiated, this means uploading the sound files from the digital recorder into their laptops and using special software to analyze each segment. They were both wearing headphones and staring at their computer screens with rapt attention.

Every now and then, one of them would look up with a start and have the other take a turn at their headphones to see if they were in agreement about what they had found. After having spent over five hours at the granary, they would probably need to spend at least 10 hours reviewing the digital recordings, another hour uploading and examining photos, and – if they had been running video cameras during their investigation – they could add another ten or fifteen hours of review time.

Kathy had often thought that there would be a lot more paranormal investigators if it hadn't been for all of that work to do afterwards! But, in some ways, the evidence review was the most exciting part. Catching a spirit's voice or image was one of the most exhilarating things she had ever experienced. It just never got old.

"Listen to this!" Bill sounded excited. "We got Poston on tape!"

"Really?" She pulled off her earphones and crossed over to pull on the pair he was holding out to her. "When? What did he say?"

"Just listen!" He scooted off his chair and invited her to sit in front of his monitor to observe the sound wave pattern that mapped what she was listening to. "Ready?"

Kathy nodded. She listened for only a few moments before her mouth dropped open. "Could you loop that? I'd like to listen to it a couple of times."

"Gotcha'"

"I can't frickin' believe this!" She squealed. "Justine is going to flip out when she hears this!"

"I know! Heck, I'm pretty jazzed about it, myself! Okay, let me back in there and I'll save that segment as a new file. We've still got a lot to listen to before we can say we're done."

She slipped out of the chair and wrapped her arms around Billy for a huge hug of congratulations. They shared a brief kiss and settled back down to work at their separate stations.

"I'm going to take a break from this and upload all of the photos. Can you pass me the camera?"

"Here you go." Bill passed the camera and the upload cord across the table. "I don't think we got much. I was scanning through the images throughout the night."

"You never know. Having a big screen can make all of the difference in what you'll find."

While waiting for the photos to finish uploading, Kathy filled two glasses with iced tea and brought them over to the table. Billy – already isolated beneath his headphones – took a long gulp and gave her a thumb's up.

31 JOSIAH RETURNS

The granary was buzzing with talk of the visitors when Josiah finally returned.

"What did they want?" He had wanted to know. "What did they do?"

Because he always stopped off in the cellar first, Dangling Will was waiting anxiously for his turn to talk. Now, more than ever his limitations chafed at him. "Why can't I be free to leave this place? Haven't I been here long enough to pay my penance for an act carried out as a result of my grief?"

"Josiah!" He exclaimed when he saw him after so long an absence. "I suppose you have heard about the messengers?"

"Yes. If that is truly what they were. . ."

"They came with machines, Josiah!! And, when I waved my hand in front of them once or twice I could answer many of their questions."

"I thought you had been seen by the girl. Couldn't she see you last night?"

"I wanted to show myself to her, but I couldn't. They were together and standing so close. . ."

"Ah. So, you wait for a hundred years to speak with the 'messenger,' and then, when she is standing right in front of you. . ."

"They said they would be back! By the time they left they understood that I am trapped here and that I want to be free. They are coming back! They said they might be able to help. . ."

"Oh, William." Josiah said consolingly. "Think about this. How can a pair of living children – for that is what they were – hope to lessen sentence imposed by

God? Do you really believe that?"

William looked at his feet. "I have hope, Josiah. For the first time in a hundred years, I have hope. Please, let me believe that there is a way to end my suffering? I lived an honorable life; raised a God-fearing son. . . Is there not room for even one failure to obey – no matter how grave?"

"That is not for either of us to say." Josiah answered softly. "My hope is that they can help you, William. I will stand by you in either case. The light waits for me at the dawn of each day, and yet I stay. If I could send you in my stead, I would. I am content to stay here among the living. I stay, and cannot imagine leaving while you can think of nothing else. In that way, I suppose death is not so different than life -- yearning for that which you cannot have."

"I taught my son of a merciful and forgiving God."

"A God with only one clear boundary over which you crossed."

"Crossed, yes! But in a moment of such deep

despair! How can there be no forgiveness for a wretched act I committed in the throes of such agony of spirit?"

"That is not for us to know. Until then, do your best to be content with your lot. Hell fire and damnation is what was promised to any who took their own lives, William." Josiah laid a hand on his shoulder. "Perhaps being imprisoned here is evidence of His mercy and forgiveness?"

Dangling Will turned to stare, dejectedly out of his window. "I have thought the same thing many times."

"Is it so bad here? The woman is hoping to transform this place into an art gallery. Just think of the things you will see and hear!"

"Yes. I am guessing she'll have to start here."

They both looked, balefully, at the pile of roofing material that draped the broken beam.

32 SNOOPY DOG

On a particularly slow Wednesday, Arthur sat behind his desk examining a paperweight he had examined a million times before. It was one of the few items he had on display for under $300.00. It wasn't an antique – as far as he knew – but, it was a pretty thing; one of those acrylic domes with assorted wildflower blossoms trapped inside, forever in their youth. At last, he set it down and pushed back from the desk.

Ever since the day he had discovered Justine collapsed in a heap on the third floor landing, he had been toying with the idea of having a little look around upstairs. He could always say he had just been making sure that the building was safe, right? The homeless riff-raff had been known to break in on occasion, and besides, he'd always wanted to know more about his luscious landlady. . .

Checking his watch, he decided that he might as well close for the day. Nobody ever showed up after 3:00 p.m. (or any other time – if he had to be honest). The café wouldn't be opening until 4:30 p.m. for the dinner crowd, so that gave him a nice window of time to poke around. The thought of sneaking around Justine's room gave him goosebumps. He smiled, mischievously, and pulled out his keys to lock the heavy wooden door that wasn't much over 6' tall.

Everyone was shorter in those days. He thought. *I've got that dining room set in the shop that looks as though it would be more at home in a Hobbit mound!*

He walked around to the café entrance and pulled the correct key from the ring to coax open the door. Justine would be pleased to see that everything had been wiped clean and made ready for the evening rush. He grabbed a bottle of Coke from the display unit and screwed off the top as he headed towards the back to climb the stairs.

The building started to close in around him and he had to shake off a feeling of dread as he approached the second floor landing.

It's broad daylight, for chrissakes! He chided himself. *The scariest thing I'm likely to run into up here is one of her damnable cats.*

But, as he rounded the corner to confront the narrow aisle of refuse that led to her bathroom and sleeping quarters, Arthur could have sworn he heard footsteps coming up behind him. Twice, he turned to check, and twice he found nothing but the empty floorboards and the dark room he'd left behind.

The tiny bathroom was populated with little sample bottles of mouthwash and hand lotion. The medicine cabinet was empty – which is always a good sign when snooping on a potential lover. He checked his reflection in the ancient mirror and smoothed back his hair.

I am one handsome devil! He grinned. *How*

could any woman resist? I ask you!

He had been tugging at his vest and straightening his tie when a sudden series of loud noises caused him to jump and let out a little yelp of terror.

Turning to look, he was relieved to see that it was only a landslide of stacked items that he had probably caused by brushing up against something as he passed.

How can any human being live like this; let alone, a woman! He clucked, picking up the items and stacking them in a fair approximation of where they had been before. *She should rent a decent apartment until she has had a chance to get this properly restored! My God! The building isn't even heated! And, this bathroom?* Arthur turned the handle on the faucet and was not surprised to see the dark brown water that burst out in a spray of protest. *Just shameful.*

Though his heart was still beating a bit too fast from his last scare, he turned to proceed further into Justine's bedroom. He fingered the luxurious fabric of her quilt and lifted a corner of it to his cheek. On a whim, he stretched out on her bed and buried his face into her pillow, trying to catch a whiff of her scent. It was a good bed – king-sized. Plenty of room for the both of them.

Her bedside table was the next thing to catch his attention. *Aha! I'll bet anything that's where she keeps her little "appliances,"* he chuckled, reaching to open the top drawer.

Just as he was about to peek into the drawer, he felt as though he was being watched, and took a guilty look around the room.

What the hell?

A mist was forming at the foot of the bed. Arthur blinked and wiped his eyes. He squinted and shook his head, but the mist was there, alright. Not only there, but growing thicker, taking shape. . .

"**You have no business here, little man.**" A voice boomed inside his head.

"Who's there? What is this all about? Are you trying to scare me? I am a proprietor here, and I. . ."

As the mist continued to take form, Arthur could see a man's angry face glowering at him in the near darkness of the room.

"I. . . I. . .was just about leave. . .I. . . I. . .was just checking to see that . . . I'm going now."

Not knowing how he did it, Arthur jumped to his feet and scurried past the apparition towards the only exit. His bowels loosened and his bladder let go, simultaneously, as he stumbled his way down the stairs, across the diner, out the door and straight into his new Passat. Without giving the upholstery a second thought, he revved the engine and took off towards parts unknown.

Somewhere, in the depths of the building, Josiah laughed.

33 WELCOME HOME

Martha went around to the passenger side of her old green Pinto to help Justine to her feet.

"Ahh! Home again!" Justine took in a deep breath and looked up at her granary. "It's still standing, I see." She laughed.

Justine took a few quick steps towards the building and stumbled.

"Not so fast!" Martha warned. "Here, let me help you."

Martha took her arm gently and guided her up the three steps to the café entrance before ushering her through the door.

"Surprise!!"

A crowd of people got to their feet and cheered when they saw Justine, and she had been glad of someone to lean on when the shock ran through her.

"Welcome home!" came from a hundred places at once, and Justine felt the tears threatening to spill down her cheeks.

"Thank you! Thank you, so much! I'm glad to be home."

She scanned the room for faces she knew, and found a good many of those, but was amazed at how many perfect strangers were smiling back at her. *Where did all of these people come from?* She wondered. Then, her eyes fell upon a large cake that had been made to resemble the granary, and the tears came on – full force.

Justine was invited to sit in a chair that had been festooned with balloons and crepe paper into a makeshift throne. There were gifts to open, and each one of them more amazing than the last; all of them geared towards helping her with the renovation of the building. One card held a promise for 8 hours of free electrical work; another, a gift card for Home Depot. . . There was a drill; a nail gun; a circular saw. . .

"This is just too wonderful! I can't believe it's real! Somebody please pinch me!"

Just as she was starting to tire, good old Martha piped up and made an announcement that could probably be heard from a block away.

"Okay, everybody! I need to get the patient up to bed! Janice and Shelby, stay behind and tidy up a bit, will you? Everybody else – OUT!"

The crowd began to shuffle out of the café in a continued state of good humor, shouting their goodbye's and well-wishes as they moved through the door.

Justine put a hand to her forehead and sent up a quiet thanks to the Lord above and all of His heavenly hosts for people like Martha. She didn't think she had ever been as exhausted as she was at this moment. Her head was pounding, and there was a thin film of sweat on her face and neck.

"I'll be right back, honey." Martha called from the doorway. "Let me get your bags from the car and lock it up, then we'll get you up to bed."

"Thanks, again, Martha."

The floor around her feet was littered with wrapping paper and ribbons; the sight of all those gifts stacked high against one wall made her feel dizzy. She yawned and stretched as well as her cast would allow and then narrowed her eyes as they tried to focus on a shadowy shape across the room. She felt a brief flash of recognition before shaking it away as just another sign of exhaustion.

"What's wrong, Justine? Are you feeling okay?" Martha had hurried into the room and was at her side in seconds.

"Oh, Martha. I think I'm losing it." She laughed. "Let's see if we can get these old bones up to bed before I collapse."

"Okay, honey. Careful. That's good."

Together, they disappeared into the stairwell.

Off in a corner of the room stood Josiah, with his arms crossed over his chest and a puzzled expression on his face. Had she seen him? He somehow believed that she had.

34 ANXIOUS TO SHARE

After having gathered all of the evidence from their investigation at the granary, Kathy and Billy arranged to meet with Justine to show her what they had found. Kathy could barely conceal her excitement on the long ride to Frederick. Billy, at the wheel, was doing a good job of seeming nonchalant about the whole deal, but Kathy suspected that was all for show.

"She is going to die when she hears this!!"

"God! I hope not." Billy chided.

"Okay. Right. Well, she is going to totally wet her pants, then. Is that better?"

He laughed. "Maybe from your point of view."

"C'mon. This is great stuff! Her ghost talked to us! Real words!"

"They talk to us all the time..."

She sighed. "Yes, but... "

"I know. You're right to be all pumped up about this. We never have a digital recorder on hand when one of them pops into our rooms in the middle of the night, or shows up in the high-school stairwell... "

Now, Kathy laughed and finished his thought. "Or, in the men's room of a McDonald's!®"

Billy felt their shared laughter as an affirmation of their love and their decision to share their lives together. He pulled his eyes away from the road just long enough to catch her radiant profile, and knew that this moment would be one of many to be forever engraved upon his heart. Her hair was thick and the color of dark chocolate. She always complained about how wavy it was, but he loved the way it bounced and lifted in the slightest breeze. He was pretty sure that he had the best girl in the entire universe. Billy was a lucky guy.

Kathy was a no-nonsense girl. She could wear makeup as well as any other woman, but often chose not to in favor of a clean, natural glow. She didn't jack a guy around with games and drama. With Kathy it was "What you see is what you get." If he didn't want her true feelings on any subject he just wouldn't ask her in the first place.

"I am anxious to meet this woman, I'll say that."

"Because of those sexy paintings in her bedroom?" She pretended to pout.

"Sure." He hadn't been able to resist. "But, mostly because of the way she has captured your imagination. You've got her down as a cross between a fairy princess, locked up forever in some ivory tower -- to a tragic heroine in some paperback romance novel. . ."

"Oh, stop. I just said that she is beautiful and mysterious."

"Same thing."

"Uh huh. You'll see."

Ten minutes later, they pulled into the tiny lot behind the granary and jumped out of the van. Kathy grabbed the laptop bag and tugged at her shirt with the free hand. "Do I look okay?" she asked with a worried look on her face.

Billy laughed out loud and took the laptop bag out of her hand.

"The most 'okay-looking' girl I've ever seen."

It was probably 32 degrees in the lot, and Billy thought the rosiness it brought to her cheeks was adorable. He planted a kiss on each cheek and whispered into her ear.

"Ready? Let's do this thing!"

Together, they navigated the icy patches on the cobblestone path and started towards the entrance.

Billy was surprised when Kathy stopped suddenly and looked up.

"Can you see him?"

He raised his eyes to the window on the top

floor and saw a man around the age of 40 with the saddest eyes he had ever seen.

"Yes."

Kathy raised her hand and waved, "Hello" to Dangling Will Poston.

35 THE "REVEAL"

Justine had seen the van pull up and had been waiting, anxiously, for the kids to come inside. Kathy had hinted at some spectacular evidence and she could hardly wait to see what they had found.

What are they doing out there? She adjusted the sling that supported her cast. No matter what she did, it seemed to want to cut a groove into her shoulder.

The café door did not hold insulated glass, and gusts of cold air penetrated the cracks and crevices around the threshold enough to give her a chill, so Justine opted to wait at a table about halfway through the room for them to arrive.

After waiting for several long minutes, their young faces could be seen peering through the door into the café. She stood and waved, calling out "Come in, it's unlocked!" as she crossed the room to the door.

"Hi!" Billy held the door for Kathy, and that made Justine smile. "This is Bill Fische, my fiancé. Bill, this is Justine Fournier."

"Justine is fine. We don't need last names around here."

"Great to meet you, Justine. Kathy has told me all about you."

"Good things, I hope?"

"Only the best things, of course." Billy turned on his charm.

"Where should we set up? Are you comfortable down here, or should we go up to the music room?"

Justine indicated a circular table in the rear of the café, and Billy walked over to set up the laptop.

"Is there an outlet?" He asked.

"Sure is. Just shift that little bookshelf with the board games on it. You'll see it."

"Ah! Yes, I do. Thanks."

"Honey, would you mind getting that shawl off the coat rack over there? I'm feeling chilly."

"Not at all." Kathy replied, bringing the intricately patterned shawl to Justine.

"Thanks.." Two attempts at draping the thing across her shoulders failed miserably, though, so Kathy took it from Justine and wrapped it around for her.

"Ah. Much better." With only a little difficulty balancing, Justine rose from her chair and moved to the one they had pulled aside for her.

"This is so exciting!" She said. "I've been dying to see what you found."

"Well, it's not so much what you'll see. . . It's more of a hearing type of thing." Billy explained.

"We did get a few interesting photos, too." Kathy added, as she loaded the DVD they had prepared.

The screen came alive with the introduction that they had prepared. Justine watched as photos of her beloved building appeared next to scrolling text that told a brief history of the building, the street address, and the date of the investigation.

"These are the photos we told you about. Notice the large glowing orbs above our heads in each one?"

"Wow. Do you think that was a ghost following you around?"

Each photo panned in to show the orbs in full detail. They were very large, and had rings around them that were vivid colors of blue, purple, and orange.

"There is a lot of debate about orbs and whether or not they are paranormal in nature. Most skeptics say that they are caused by dust in the air, or bugs. . ."

"But, these are so big!"

"Exactly." Kathy agreed, her eyes on the screen. "We wouldn't have brought them to you if we hadn't thought these were unusual enough to share. I mean, why would a dust particle follow us through this huge building? "

"Ah." Justine pointed at the current photo as it panned in towards a close-up view. "That one was taken on the top floor by that back window."

"Yep."

"And, there, that was taken on the third floor. . ."

"Right."

"Wow."

"We agree."

"Okay. Kathy whispered. Watch this!"

A screen shot of a wavy sound file filled the screen. A cursor moved to hit the play button and they all sat – transfixed – listening as the file played.

"Why do you stay here in the granary?" It was Kathy's voice, Justine knew. Then, there was a deeper voice. . . she thought she might have heard something, but. . . :

"Keep watching," Kathy urged.

The cursor selected the area that had been so hard to hear, and then selected a function called "Amplify" from a pull down menu along the top of the screen. Again, they sat on the edge of their seats, listening for the ghostly answer to Kathy's question.

"Why do you stay here in the granary?" It played Kathy's voice again.

"God is punishing me for what I did."

Justine held her breath. She felt a little faint.

"Play that again!" She demanded

"It will, it will. Just listen, here it comes again."

The DVD had been set up to play each EVP four times. Once, at normal volume, and three times with the spirit's voice amplified.

Justine knew that her mouth was hanging open, but she couldn't seem to get a grip on her astonishment.

"He spoke to you."

"Yep."

"Listen! There's more!"

"More?"

"Shh. Here we go. EVP number 2"

"How many are there?" Justine asked in a hushed whisper.

"Eleven!" Kathy chirped with a huge smile.

"Eleven?"

36 HELLO?

She watched the van pull away with mixed feelings. The voice that had been recorded on the fourth floor had sounded so sad and lonely. She wondered how many times he had watched her as she pulled supplies off the stacks that were stored there. Some of the footsteps that she could hear as she laid awake in bed late at night were probably his. She turned her back on the drafty entrance door and leaned against it. The cold glass was welcome, as it soothed and grounded her from all of the tumult of knowledge that was waging war with her heart.

Though it had been a very long day, and she ached all over, Justine braced herself for what she knew she must do next. Her hand wiped a tear from her cheek, and she straightened to pull away from the blessed reality of the icy door. It wasn't as if she could go on walking around him, now that she knew he was trapped up there – all alone.

With stern resolve she marched up the seemingly-endless stairs to the fourth floor. Once at the top, she paused only a moment before striding over to his corner of the room. She hadn't been back here since her fall, and was dismayed all over again at the sight of the caved in ceiling beam.

I am going to have to get somebody out here tomorrow. She thought, wondering how in the hell she was going to pay anyone to fix it.

Justine walked over to the window where William Poston had spent the last century waiting to be set free.

"Hello? Mr. Poston?"

Her voice was barely audible, and she felt ridiculous talking to the empty room, but she continued, regardless. It was something she felt she had to do if she were to go on sharing a home with him.

"You know me well enough by now to know that I can't see or hear you." She paused, suddenly exhausted, and leaned against the windowsill before continuing. "The kids that were here to speak to you last week? They just played me a recording of your voice. I was able to hear you for the very first time, Mr. Poston. I just wanted to come straight up here to you and tell you that I'm sorry my home has been your prison all these years. I may not be able to hear you or see you, but I do know that you are here with me, and I promise that I will come up and visit with you sometimes. Maybe, someday, I'll even be able to see you?"

She nudged some of the debris at her feet, and kept her head down.

"Anyway. Don't be so sad, okay?" She stopped herself just as she was about to say that 'life was too short.'

"Okay. I'm going to bed now. Good night."

Still feeling pretty silly about this late-night ghost encounter, Justine raised her hand in a half-hearted goodbye wave and turned to leave.

"Good night." A faint voice came from behind her.

She stopped mid-stride.

Did I really hear that? No. No. I'm just over tired.

Not entirely convinced that she wasn't losing her marbles, Justine navigated the cavernous building to her quiet haven of a bedroom where she fell, fully-dressed, into a deep and dreamless sleep.

37 POUFY SHIRT

Kathy and Bill pulled away from the building and headed for home. The van was freezing cold inside, and they were both shivering in the frigid wheezing puffs that were the van's excuse for heat until it warmed up for thirty minutes.

"Brrrr!"

"Hungry?" Billy asked, turning left at the intersection.

"I could eat." She replied

"Who is open this late?"

"7-11?"

"Is there one around here?"

"Yep. Take a right where that Volkswagen just turned in."

"So. Did you see him?"

"Who? The guy in the poufy shirt?"

"You did! Why didn't you say anything?"

"Why didn't you say anything?"

He took his eyes off the road long enough to share a long look with her.

"I figured that Justine woman had enough to chew on for one night."

"Yeah."

"Here it is!" He said, pulling into the 7-11's parking lot and taking a space right in front of the door.

"Told you so." She quipped.

They jumped out of the car and ran inside to choose some snacks for the road. Kathy's first stop was a cup of hot cocoa, while Bill made a beeline to the fridge for a Diet Coke. They met in the cookie aisle after that where they picked up a bag of chocolate chip cookie to share.

Later, while munching cookies and sipping on their drinks, Kathy brought up the topic of the apparition again.

"Do you think he knew?"

"Nope."

"Why not?"

"He was too absorbed in what we had to show Justine, and besides, why should he worry about us? As far as he knows, we are just as oblivious as everybody else who comes through that place."

"I wonder who he was?"

"We would have to ask him. That place has got too much history to isolate every person who died in it."

"True."

"So? What should we do about him? Think we

should tell her?"

"Nope." This answer was followed by a brief period of contemplative chewing.

"Is there anything we can do to help Will?" Kathy asked.

"Your guess is as good as mine on that score. Maybe he's right where he's supposed to be."

Kathy let go of a heavy sigh and sipped her tepid cocoa.

"I just hate to think of him sitting there for another century or two. Don't you?"

"Maybe he should have thought of that before he... "

"Don't say it . . . C'mon, Billy. He wasn't in his right mind when he did that. I really think he has suffered enough."

"Ha. That's not for you to say, though, is it?"

"Well, regardless, I am going to sit down and research this punishment thing on the net and see if anybody has any theories on the subject."

"Can't hurt." He answered, dubiously. "Don't see how it can help, either. . . but,"

Kathy crossed her arms in a body posture Bill knew only too well.

"Tell you what, I don't hold out much hope, but I'll work with you to see what we can find."

Kathy's arms dropped to her sides and she accepted the hand that he offered. Her hand rested comfortably inside his all the rest of the way home; even after she dropped off to sleep with her head against the window and her lips slightly parted.

Billy stole occasional glances at her as she slept. He had heard about people who were "of one mind," but felt that was more than a saying when it came to the two of them. They had both seen the ghost standing over Justine; had both chosen not to acknowledge its presence for the same reasons, and simultaneously agreed not to share the story with Justine.

He worked his hand free of hers very carefully and scratched an itchy place on his nose.

How many people could find a partner who joined with them so seamlessly? Billy smiled and took up her hand again.

Kathy stirred at his touch, but didn't wake. A gentle snow began to dust the windshield and dance through the beams of their headlights. The white van rolled down the highway with an almost reverential silence towards home.

38 BAD CASTING

After six tortuous weeks of un-scratchable itches and difficult, one-armed showers, it was finally time to have the cast removed from her left arm. Justine sat in the Orthopedist's office in a state of exultant anticipation; waiting for Dr. Ichtaz to show up with his electric pizza-cutter thingy and set her free.

While she waited, she turned her arm this way and that to examine all of the signatures that had been squiggled across every available inch of it.

I should have gone down the stairs on my face years ago! She mused, not for the first time.

Since her tumble, café business had increased

ten-fold, and the people that she had always thought of as "regulars," had blossomed into dear friends. In addition, there had been so many offers to help her with the renovations that she had been able to make unbelievable progress on the building in a very short time; and the gifts and donations she had received had been jaw-droppingly generous.

Justine remembered the nights preceding the accident, and the many tears she had shed due to the crushing isolation and the overwhelming task she had set for herself with the granary. Though she knew that giving up would never have been an option, but the limits of her strength and resources had taken a mighty toll.

She ran her finger over Martha's rolling signature and smiled. She had a strong and steady hand, with generous loops and swirls that spoke of her solid and open nature. Memories of Martha's stalwart care and protection throughout the ordeal brought a sentimental smile to her face. She had been a much-needed mother figure.

Justine sighed. Her mother. She had never

even told her mother about the accident. Martha had frowned on her decision to keep the incident from her family, but Justine knew that her mom would have piled the broken arm and bashed-in head on top of all of her other arguments to just "sell the rat trap and come home," and she hadn't wanted to give her family any more ammunition.

The Dr. knocked lightly on the door before entering, and came in with his customary good humor.

"Justine. Are you ready to have this cast off, young lady?" He beamed.

"So ready. You can't begin to imagine." She answered, slipping her arm out of the sling and offering it up to his examination.

"My, my! Got a few friends, haven't you?"

She laughed. "Apparently. But, who knew?"

"Well, we will be very careful not to damage it too much getting it off of you."

"You'd better! This has already been

appropriated for exhibit in my gallery."

He called in his assistant, Audrey, and they proceeded to saw the cast from her arm.

"Now, remember, this arm has been out of the sunlight and unused for a very long time. It will be pale and very weak. Muscles that aren't in use quickly degenerate, so you are going to have to attend your physical therapy sessions and do daily repetitions of the exercises they assign you before you will be able to achieve the full range of motion."

"I'll probably be too busy scratching it to worry about what it looks like." She said, only half-joking.

"They do itch something fierce, don't they?"

With deft hands, Dr. Ichtaz lifted the cast from her arm and Justine was free of the darn thing.

"Ahhhh. . ." She half-moaned, half-sighed as the cool office air welcomed her suffocated arm.

"There you go. Now, let's have a look."

He moved her through several exercises and

was pleased with the result.

"Okay! Everything looks just the way it should. Tell Amy I'd like to see you again in three weeks." He beamed.

Justine jumped off the exam table and gave her arm a good, thorough scratching.

"Will do, doc. Thanks!"

She gathered up the commemorative piece of artwork that had been her cast and headed home in an especially buoyant frame of mind.

39 RAISING THE ROOF

The brother-in-law of a friend that was a neighbor of Paul Merritt (one of her new café regulars), came bright and early one Wednesday morning with an impressive tool belt hanging from his hips. Rumor had it that this guy was one of the most eligible bachelors around; single and devastatingly handsome.

I could use a man around here that is good with his hands. . . She mused as her eyes moved over him with as much discretion as she could muster. *I'll take a dish of that with whipped cream and sprinkles, thank you very much.*

"You must be my roofer." Justine said, holding out her hand in greeting. "Am I ever glad to see you!"

Mark took her hand and shook it briefly. "I am!

He laughed. "I hear you have a bit of a mess upstairs."

"That we do. Follow me, and I'll introduce you to the mess."

They started for the stairwell, when Justine stopped and returned to lock the café door and flip the "Open" sign to "Closed." It felt kind of thrilling to lock the guy in. . . .

Shame on me.

He was shorter than her by a few inches, but the man was all muscles and watching him move could have fascinated her for hours. His eyes were a deep blue; his hair was a rich, dark brown that curled this way and that in a provocative play of light. It looked soft. *So soft.*

"Okay. Here we go." She gave herself a mental cold shower. "Watch your step. Oh... And, there's no point in grabbing the handrails as they aren't attached, yet."

Mark had instinctively grabbed the handrail, and had already discovered that for himself. "Yeah. I noticed that."

Justine giggled. With the realization that she was acting like a teenager she flushed scarlet.

Grow up, Justine! He's just a man, for cripe's sake! She chided herself.

"Wow." He said, looking around at the huge, dark expanses that reached out on either side as ascended. "This building is enormous."

"It is. I have big plans for this place. But, as you can see, there is still a lot of work to be done."

"Who have you got heading up your renovations?" He asked. "United? Consolidated?"

"Me."

Their eyes met and he scratched his head – too polite to press further.

"Here we are!" She said as they reached the landing.

His eyes scanned the room – obviously looking for damage and not seeing any.

"It's way over there." She pointed off into the distance and then moved off in that direction. "Here."

"Ah. Yes. That is a mess."

Justine sighed deeply before responding. She put one hand to her forehead and grimaced. "So? What do you think? Is it fixable? Will I have to give you my first-born child?"

Mark stood there, looking up through the gaping hole in the roof. He scratched the back of his head.

"Ever thought of having a large family?" He quipped.

"No! Oh, please tell me I won't have to surrender more than one offspring!"

Mark looked at the huge beam laying there all splintered and broken.

"How did this happen?" He asked, mystified. "Doesn't look like a lightning strike; there's no rot or insect infestation, either. This beam looks as though it could hold up the entire state of Arkansas for a couple of centuries without breaking a sweat."

"I'd tell you what happened, but you wouldn't believe me." She said. "The important bit is what are we to do about fixing it?"

He stood there, with that quizzical look on his face until it had become clear that she wasn't about to satisfy his curiosity.

Then, Mark pulled out a notepad from his shirt pocket and started scribbling down notes and measurements. Justine got out of his way and leaned against the nearby windowsill. He was taking a long time to work up a total, and she was getting worried.

Finally, Mark raised his eyes from the scribbles and cleared his throat.

Justine walked back over to him and put up a hand in supplication. "Please, please, please don't take my progeny!" She joked, half-heartedly.

Mark wasn't smiling. Justine gulped.

"This isn't a small task." He started. "First, we

have to have a matching beam milled – this isn't standard stock anywhere in the world. These beams were rough-cut lumber and they are 10"x 10"s, which is . . . large."

"I don't need it to match the others. . . " She interrupted. For now, I'd be happy just to keep the weather out."

"No. That would be a mistake. This property is historic! You've got to know it would be a crime to do anything half-assed." He seemed to notice that he had just used questionable language and started to back pedal. "I'm sorry. That wasn't the most diplomatic way to. . . "

She sighed. "Actually, that was exactly the right thing to say. You're right. I love this place more than any sane person has a right to, and I want the repair to be done right."

He shifted, uncomfortably and looked at the little notepad full of scribbles.

"Tell you what." He said, a line of concentration

creasing his brows. "Let me make some phone calls and see what I can do. I promise to get back to you in a day or two with a plan of action."

He followed her gaze to the gaping hole. "Is there anything we can do in the meantime to keep the weather out?"

He considered this. "Sure. I've got a tarp on the truck. I'll get that covered up until we can figure out what to do."

She smiled. *God in heaven but you're a good looking hunk of manhood!* She thought as he returned her smile with a glint from those heart-achingly blue eyes.

"Well. That's a deal, then! Thank you for coming out, Mark. I really appreciate it more than I can say."

He started off towards the stairs and she followed, taking in the view. Thankfully, he didn't notice when she turned to wave a friendly goodbye to the empty room.

40 GREEN-EYED GHOST

Josiah huffed his annoyance over crossed arms as he leaned against one of the sturdy columns that supported the crossbeams on the fourth floor. "Think she actually liked that panty-waist?" He grumbled.

"Now, don't get yourself all jealous! She's a lonely woman, Josiah. A living woman." Will Poston shifted uneasily in the silence that followed. It didn't do to get Josiah mad at you.

"Ah. Don't I know it." Josiah sighed.

For the first time in over a century, Josiah looked uncertain; lost. It wasn't natural for him to show so much weakness, and it made Will extremely uncomfortable.

"I know you care for the girl, Josiah. You've watched over her since the moment she stepped over that threshold; and protected her, too." He added that last bit as a balm to the man's suffering.

"A man like that would be able to help her with all of this." Josiah waved his hand in a weak, horizontal arc.

"He would." Will agreed.

The ghosts shared an extended silence; Will, staring out of his window; Josiah, leaning against his column, deep in thought.

From below, the sounds of Justine's flirtatious laughter could be overheard at regular intervals. Josiah could barely hide his annoyance and would wince with each occurrence. After a particularly extended bout of giggling drifted its way up through the floorboards, Josiah stood up to his full height and growled. "She's acting like a child! What can be that funny? Tell me, Will! The woman has completely taken leave of her senses."

"What will be, will be." Intoned Poston.

Josiah raised his head with a sudden revelation.

"I've got it!" He slapped his hands together. "She's flirting to bring down the price! Of course! That's what is going on here." His posture regained its usual confidence, by degrees. "How long have we known Justine, Will? And, yet I have allowed myself to doubt her! It is obvious that she is only protecting her wallet with all of that ridiculous eyelash fluttering and cheek blushing. . ."

"Josiah, you must find a way to resolve these feelings you have for her. Whether she blushes or not is a matter for the living."

But, when he turned to look for a reply, Josiah was gone. "Leave those two to get on with their living." He muttered. "The girl needs a husband." He gazed, again, out his window and into the gathering dusk. "She does, indeed."

41 I SEE DEAD PEOPLE

As work on the roof progressed, Justine was spending more time on the fourth floor. She made a show of shifting things about, or taking inventory of her building supplies, but she thought they both knew what was really going on.

Night after long and lonely night, Justine would lay awake in bed and remember something that Mark had said or done that day; the way he had looked at the time; the way she had felt because of the way he had looked. . . It was glorious to anticipate to his sparkling blue eyes and flirtatious smiles.

She wondered if he was dating anybody special. He never spoke of it, if he was. But, though she awoke each morning hoping for an invitation to dinner and a movie, Mark made no move to change the status of their business relationship.

For a fleeting moment, she had wondered if he might be gay. But, no. That couldn't be the case! She had felt his eyes on her body, had seen the knowing smile one afternoon when she had pretended to stumble into him. On that occasion, he had placed a gentle hand on each shoulder to steady her, and their eyes had met for several long moments – long enough for her to wonder if she was about to be kissed. . .

The flirtation continued for several days, until the gap had been successfully (and seamlessly) closed in the roof, and the new beam had been positioned and secured in place. As the work neared completion, Justine began to fear that Mark was going to walk out of her life as suddenly as he had entered it.

On those last few nights, when sleep refused to come, Justine walked up the two flights to spend time "talking" with William. She had positioned an old armchair near Will's window so that she could snuggle up in her warmest robe and talk out her fears and frustrations. Though there had never been any response from the spirit, she had known that he was there, and had come to find his presence very comforting.

"William, he will be finished tomorrow. There is nothing left for him to do but gather up his ladders and tools and collect his pay."

Justine hugged her knees and rested her chin on them; the hair she usually braided or pulled back in a thick ponytail, had been set free and fell gloriously over her shoulders in loose waves.

"What should I do? What is he waiting for? I think I'm in . . ."

She tucked her face out of sight by shifting her forehead to where her chin had been.

"Okay. I know this sounds foolish – especially to a man who has been around for a couple hundred years – but, these things happen, don't they? These 'love-at-first-sight' things that we've all heard about. . ."

Justine raised her eyes and wiped the unexpected tears from her cheeks.

"What will I do if he just takes the money and walks out? How will I survive that kind of hurt, William? Oh. I wish I could see you – just once. Knowing that you're here makes me feel less alone."

The words had barely left her lips when a mist began to form between her and the window. With a sharp intake of breath, she watched as the mist gained substance. First, heavy boots appeared, followed by brown pants and a long-sleeved shirt made of linen. The figure that was coming together before her was that of a tall and exceedingly handsome man, with broad shoulders, a muscular chest, dark wavy hair, and tender eyes.

"Can you see me, Justine?" Josiah asked, in a resonant voice.

"William? Is that you?"

"No. My name is Josiah. Don't you remember me? We have danced together many times."

A sharp pang of recognition barely eluded her conscious mind. Vague images of the man before her would momentarily surface, only to be concealed behind a curtain of forgetfulness.

"After I fell?" She whispered.

"Yes."

"Ah. But, where's William? Isn't he here with us?"

"He is."

The apparition named Josiah gestured to an empty space beside him. "He is here, but is not as strong as I."

"Hello, William." She directed her voice to the empty spot, feeling as though she had slipped into a dream and wasn't sure how to go about waking up again.

"You are a strong woman. I have witnessed your fear at the prospect of losing the . . . um. . .'short' man." He said.

Josiah swung his head suddenly around and winced as though he had been jabbed by an invisible elbow.

"All I want to say is that you are not alone, Justine. You will never be alone again."

Much later, when Justine woke up in the easy chair on the fourth floor, she tried to remember what she had been dreaming. There was a man . . . no, a ghost?

Feeling chilled and wondering what time it was, she shook off her musings and – gathering her heavy robe around her for warmth – navigated her way downstairs with thoughts of a hot shower and a cup of coffee.

42 PROJECT FORGIVENESS

Kathy left for work every morning at 8:00 a.m. and didn't return to her mother's house until 6:30 p.m. She had a boring receptionist position at an architectural firm in Rockville, and had huge gaps of time between phone calls and visiting clients during which she could surf the net. Ordinarily, this led to overspending on things she would often have to return due to size, color or quality issues.

But, ever since they had heard William Poston's desperate pleas for help, she had been using that time to research "repentance" and "forgiveness" theories. The sheer volume of opinions and rhetoric around this topic had been overwhelming. Everybody seemed to have their own convictions on the subject, and every single one of them was certain that their beliefs were the only ones that could be given any credence, whatsoever.

She had always been an organized and methodical girl with a penchant for spreadsheets, so it wasn't long before she had everything from bible quotations to ancient Indian rituals catalogued and itemized for later review. Convincing Bill that there was anything that could be done to help Mr. Poston was like trying to make contact lenses for a housefly. Every time the topic came up he either took refuge in a video game or became suddenly engrossed in a book.

One evening, as they were sitting in Billy's apartment working on seating plans for their wedding reception, Kathy pulled a sheaf of pages out of a folder and shoved them under his nose.

"What's this?" It took him a few minutes to cipher out what the columns and numbers were trying to get across. "Kathy." He rested a hand on her shoulder and let out a heavy sigh. "You need to let this go."

"Just read it!"

"Kathy."

"Okay, then. Don't read it, Billy. Just listen to me!"

"Honey, this stuff is all superstition and religious hullaballoo. "

"Like ghosts?" She asked, eyeing him sideways.

Billy placed the spreadsheets gently on the glass surface of the coffee table, and shifted his position on the sofa to face her.

"Okay. So, you've done a lot of work here. I can see that this means a lot to you. Now, what is it that you think we should do?"

Excited now that she had his full attention, Kathy took both of his hands in hers and started to lay out a plan of action. A series of expressions – from consternation to wonder and back again – passed across Billy's face. When he thought she had finished, he shook h is head and appraised his wife-to-be.

"I'm in love with a crazy person." He said, matter-of-factly.

"Well, maybe." Kathy admitted. "But, what could it hurt? Don't you think it's at least worth a try?"

"Um."

"Oh, c'mon! I promised him I would try to help him get out of that place and back with his son where he belongs!"

"But. . ."

Kathy's pretty mouth turned down in an irresistible pout. He had never been able to withstand the power of her pout and she knew it. Billy gathered his love into his arms and kissed her neck before seeking out her luscious lips. At the very last moment, though, she had dodged his kiss and turned her pouting head away.

"Sweetie?"

"What."

"I was just going to tell you that I would never let you be crazy all by yourself."

"Really?" The pouty mouth was still in effect, but her eyes were interested in what he had just said.

Thinking that he had never seen a funnier little face in all of his natural born days, he moved in for another kiss. This time, she grudgingly allowed it.

"But, Kathy?"

"Uh huh?"

"Where are you going to get the other 48 crazy people?"

"Where there's a Bill there's a way!" She quipped.

Billy rolled his eyes and groaned.

43 HE LOVES ME. HE LOVES ME NOT

Justine tried to be optimistic as she scrambled dozens of eggs and fried bacon for the morning breakfast crowd. Her days had a rhythm that could carry her through hard times and heartbreaks. At least, they had always done so in the past. . .

Her apron pocket held a certified check in the amount of $2,650.00. It represented her entire savings account, and it was made out to Mark Mattson.

Justine Mattson. Her subconscious tried the name on for size.

He would walk in that door sometime today and start to carry out his tools, sawhorses, and ladder. He had never asked for her number; never offered to take her to dinner. Now, his work was done, and he was going to just load up his truck and drive away.

With her heart soaring one minute and sinking the next, the morning passed very slowly. A snow storm was predicted for later, and, as a result, her lunch crowd was more like a 'lunch bunch.' The check was heavy in her pocket. She thought of spritzing it with her perfume, but managed to bring her teenage side under control in the end.

This was a business transaction! She kept remonstrating herself. *He gave me a bargain-basement price and did an excellent job, and he deserves every penny. He never led me on, or made promises to. . .*

Justine's imagination finished her thought. She blushed at the images she was capable of calling to mind when it came to thoughts of the two of them together. His calloused hands caressing her body; his fevered kisses; her passion set free after so many years.

How would she bear losing him? What if he just took the check from her and waved goodbye? For weeks, he had been her reason for getting out of bed in the morning. She had caught herself singing silly love songs at odd moments, and her daydreams had been full of Mark. Did he have any feelings for her? Had she made too much of his winks and smiles; his witty remarks and the way he had of "accidentally" brushing up against her and grinning an apology?

At 3:00 p.m., she climbed the stairs and did her best to freshen-up. After much consideration, she decided to allow her hair to flow freely down her back. Never one to wear cosmetics, she pinched some color into her cheeks and practiced thanking him for an excellent job in front of the cracked bathroom mirror.

By 4:00, she had already spent thirty minutes pacing the café floor. The tables had all been polished to a shine, the floor had been swept, and she had checked her reflection in the downstairs restroom a dozen times. She walked to peer out the front windows now, for any signs of his approach, then, lifted each arm in turn to sniff her armpits.

The storm had come through at 5:30 p.m. and,

within an hour, had pretty much closed the streets for the night. Justine's feet ached and the emotional roller-coaster she had been riding all day had finally taken its toll. With a heavy sigh, she flipped the "Closed" sign so that it would face the street, locked everything up tightly, and climbed the steps to her room.

A sudden fear gripped her and she needed to run all the way up to the top of the building to make sure Mark's tools were still there.

They were.

"He never showed." She said to the empty room. *"And, he never called. And, I'm very tired and I'm going to bed. Good night, William."*

Justine hesitated. What was that dream ghosts' name? Joseph? James? Joshua? It was something that started with a "J."

"And, good night, Mr. J." She added.

.

4 GUARDIAN AND PROTECTOR

Josiah followed Justine to her room. Sadness trailed behind her like the tattered and soiled train of a wedding dress that had never fulfilled its purpose. Her head was bowed, and her hair was unbound and uncharacteristically tangled.

He wanted to touch her; soothe her, but knew that his was not the caress that she longed for. As each item of clothing fell away from her body, she emerged more vulnerable and forlorn. The sterling silver, boar's hair brush lay untouched on her bedside table. Josiah knew that she brushed her hair to a glossy shine before dropping off to sleep most nights, and found himself wishing that she would perform this life-affirming act to reassure him of her ability to move forward as she always had in the past.

In all of the years Josiah had observed her from the shadows, he had never seen her look so defeated. It frightened him.

Tears -- or even a good temper tantrum would have been preferable to this cloak of hopelessness, rejection and abandonment that she had wrapped herself in. How could a lioness like Justine have been brought low by such a brainless bundle of muscles in a tool belt? The man was so clearly unworthy of such a reaction.

I've a good mind to chase that coward down and drag him back by his hair.

The anger simmered within him, but could not come to a boil. That was the thing about being dead — you just couldn't maintain a healthy seethe. Besides, he was needed here.

As soon as Justine had found refuge in a deep sleep, Josiah moved to sit beside her on the bed. He picked up her brush and gently worked it through her hair; picking up small sections, smoothing the tangles and snarls, then laying each aside to take up the next.

Josiah had never married. Female companionship had been nothing more than a pleasant pastime during his lifetime, and there had been no shortage of willing females. His days had been squandered in the pursuit of wealth and property, and his purchase of the granary and been one of his crowning achievements. At the time of his death in 1890, he had been one of the most successful businessmen in Maryland.

Memories of the fire flashed before him for the first time in many years. He had been on the top floor of the granary, supervising a particularly large delivery of wheat from Virginia, when he had first noticed the smell of smoke as it wafted up through the floor boards and filled the stairwells. Though he had made every effort to gain control of his panicked workers, bedlam had prevailed. A group of men had devised a plan to lower themselves into the silos via heavy lengths of rope in order to gain access to the lower levels and find an exit. For the first three men down the rope, it had proved a wise undertaking, and they had managed to escape the flames and smoke to live another day. But, any who followed after were met with certain death as the fire had been smoldering deep beneath the grain for some time and would burst into flames as these last were making their descent.

Many had thrown open the windows and jumped to their deaths on the cobbles below. Josiah knew that the open air had only served to feed the flames, but his cries had not been heard over the roaring of the fire as it feasted with unbridled gluttony on the heavy beams that surrounded them.

Gasping for air, Josiah had been drawn to the promise of fresh air that the open windows, promised, when the floor had given way and served him up as a sacrifice to the inferno below. His last intake of breath had invited the searing flames into his nose, throat and lungs to deliver their agonizing gift of death.

Every morning since, when he turned from the wall of brilliant light that beckoned him towards a new beginning, he was repelled by the memories of his last moments of agony, and saddened by the life he had lived and the choices he had made. Now -- when it could bring no joy to either of them -- he had lost himself in love.

William is right. He ran both hands through is hair. *She needs a husband; one who can share her dreams and ease her burdens; a man who is still full of life and strength. What am I but a shadow on her wall? How could I ever hope to be any more than that?*

Though ghosts never sleep, Josiah stretched out beside her on the king-sized bed and lost himself in reflections of days gone by.

45 THE MORNING AFTER

"Hello." Her greeting to him upon waking had come as quite a shock. Josiah sat up and immediately began to fade out of sight.

"You don't have to go. It's Josiah, isn't it? Your name? I couldn't remember it last night. . ."

He fought the urge to disappear, and was only able to maintain a flickering image before her tousled gaze.

"So. . . Do we sleep together every night? Or, is this something new?"

She sat there – naked from the waist up -- with the sheets loosely draped across her thighs. Her face was wearing a sardonic grin, and she made no move to cover her breasts, which, damn them, had drawn his gaze and taken it hostage.

"My eyes are up here." She chided, playfully, pointing at her face. "So, men are the same dead or alive! It's true what they say – we learn something new every day."

"I . . . um . . . well. . ."

"Yes? You want to say something?"

"Ghosts don't sleep." He answered sheepishly, eyes downcast. "You were . . . well. . . Last night you were. . ."

Understanding came over her face and her expression softened.

"Ah. Yes. I was a bit dramatic, wasn't I?"

"He doesn't deserve you." The words had been out of his mouth before he could stop them.

"Hmm. Yes. Nobody does, it seems."

She stood up and the sheet slipped away from her like dew from a rose. Standing there in her nakedness, she had reminded him of every beautiful thing he had lost when he died. She was so noble; so unashamed. This was the lioness he had come to expect. He regarded her with awe.

"We were concerned. We had never seen you so unhappy."

"We?" She met his eyes with the question.

"William. . . Will and me . . . myself." He dropped his forehead into his palm and groaned.

I am stuttering like an idiot! She must think I have never seen a naked woman before!

"I decided to stay until you felt more like yourself." He explained with renewed vigor. "Everyone here depends on you to stay strong."

Justine pulled her hair back and stretched, gloriously. "That's me! Strong as an ox, and just as ornery."

Without another word, she padded off to the

bathroom.

"Not an ox, at all!" He raised his voice, hesitant to follow. "More of a lioness!"

Her laughter provided a lyrical accompaniment to the sound of her urine hitting the water in the bowl. "A 'lioness,' is it, now?"

"Yes. And, I defy anyone to argue the matter!"

They laughed together, then, as lovers might have; lovers – or friends.

46 WEDDING PLANS

As Billy was impossible to nail down about wedding arrangements, Kathy had sought her mother out for help and advice. The amazing result of this collaboration was a newfound closeness and camaraderie between the two women that had been almost non-existent since Kathy had begun to speak openly about seeing "dead people," somewhere around the age of eight or nine.

Louise Harold had been heartbroken to discover that her daughter was "mentally ill," and had wasted no time in hustling Kathy off to the nearest mental health professional for evaluation. Kathy had gone willingly enough, though no punishment or medication had ever been successful in making her recant her stories of visions and conversations with spirits. Though Kathy knew that her parents loved her, she could never bring herself to deny the gifts that gave her life added depth and dimension.

When Kathy's father had run off with one of his leggy coworkers in the spring of 1983, Kathy had felt largely responsible; (a belief that her mother had made no effort to contradict). As she got older, Kathy found that her classmates and teachers did look at her sideways and go out of their ways to avoid her.

"I don't care whether or not you see spirits!" Her mother had warned many times. "Just keep it to yourself! People will think you are crazy. You will never have friends or boyfriends if you keep on that way. Don't you want to get married someday? What about children? Don't you want to have children?"

And, her mother had been right. As soon as Kathy had stopped acknowledging the spirits to others, her social life had improved remarkably. She had been dating Billy Fische for two years before he had (red-faced and covered in beads of sweat) finally confessed his abilities to her. At first, he had thought she was making fun of him by claiming to have the same gifts, but over the next several weeks, shared visions and voices convinced him that he had found someone with whom he could be fully himself without fear.

The wedding was to be held in the little church a few blocks from their homes on the same day in February that they had shared their true natures with one another. Billy was going to wear a charcoal grey tux with a deep burgundy vest and tie. Her dress was a reproduction of a Victorian wedding gown, and was a perfect complement to her curvaceous body. The bridesmaids (two cousins and her college roommate) were to wear Victorian-style dresses in a slightly lighter shade of burgundy – to bring out the color in the men's vests.

Billy's mother had accepted his ability to speak to ghosts after her only daughter, Charity, had been horribly murdered. According to Billy, he had been visited by his sister several times, and had been able to convey messages from her to his grieving parents. Still, he might never have been taken seriously if Charity had not appeared before his mother just before entering the light. The difference was that Billy had been able to develop his skills with more confidence and freedom than Kathy had been allowed.

As neither family had much money to put towards the wedding, the couple had decided to keep the ceremony simple, and the reception would be held in a tiny reception hall in the church's basement. Their cake would be made by Kathy's Aunt Pam who was flying in from Nashville the week before the wedding. Kathy had seen photos of some of Aunt Pam's creations and felt confident that whatever she made for the occasion would be both stunning and delicious.

Kathy had purchased the bride and groom cake topper in one of the quaint antique shops that lined the main street in Frederick. The ceramic couple had been waiting under an arch of finely sculpted pink roses, and Kathy had been unable to resist them. How perfect to have an antique cake decoration for a vintage-themed wedding?

To date, the invitation list numbered just under 100, with 15 of those out of town and not likely to attend.

As long as we have at least fifty in the chapel, everything should be perfect. Kathy mused. They had met with Pastor Dave the previous Wednesday and – to their mutual joy – he had not only understood their strange request, but had agreed to carry it out during the ceremony!

All they could do now was hope and pray that all would go as planned. . .

47 PAYMENT IN FULL

When Justine entered the café that morning, Martha was already at work scrambling eggs and dealing sliced bread onto cookie sheets for toasting.

"Martha! You are supposed to be enjoying your well-earned retirement; not slinging hash in some hole-in-the-wall café!"

Martha laughed, but did not look up from her work.

"I tried that retirement business, and it just wasn't for me." She stated emphatically. "Besides, this place is too much for you to manage on your own."

"Well, you may have a point there." Justine pulled on an apron and joined Martha in the kitchen.

"So? What happened? I haven't been able to think about anything else."

"What? Oh."

Justine's face said it all.

"He didn't show up, did he?"

"No. He didn't call, either."

"His stuff is still here, right?"

"Yes."

"And his check?"

"Sure is."

"Well, maybe he'll show up today."

Justine let out a heavy sigh and pulled a five-pound package of bacon out of the fridge.

"Oh, Martha. I don't know. Maybe I just imagined that something was happening between us?"

"No. I saw you two kibitzing around each other like a couple of foals in a field."

"Really? So, you saw it, too?"

"Of course, I saw it! Don't know how anybody could have missed that flirty word play and batting of eyelashes."

"Oh, jeez. Now, I feel like a total idiot."

"Don't you know by now that everybody in this place loves you and wants to see you happy?"

Justine smiled and started peeling strips of bacon off the package and dropping them onto the grill.

"I guess they've proved that. But, I didn't know we were being so obvious."

"Ha."

"But, if he has feelings for me, then why the cold shoulder now?"

"Don't worry so much, honey. He'll probably show up today with a great excuse, and you guys can just pick up where you left off."

"What excuse can anybody have for not calling? Especially these days, when everybody and their brother owns a cell phone."

"Trust me. Old Martha has lived a long time and has seen her share of men with commitment issues."

"Do you think that's it? He's afraid of getting too serious?"

"Who knows? But, if that was his problem, it wouldn't be unusual. Guys don't get to be his age and single unless they have a pretty sophisticated line of defenses."

Having laid out four rows of bacon and turned on the grill, Justine went to unlock the door and flip the "Closed" sign around. People were already waiting outside with hungry looks on their faces, and they came in from the cold, gratefully, stomping the snow off of their boots before finding a table and sitting down.

Justine grabbed her abdomen and grimaced

with an all-too-familiar cramp in her side. Though often quite painful, they always passed quickly, so she dismissed them as muscle cramps probably caused by the amount of lifting and physical labor she engaged in on a daily basis.

Most of their morning patrons were not able to pay for their breakfasts. The café more than made up for this loss with the lunch and dinner crowd, though. They were mostly comprised of local business owners who were willing to pay more for their food in the interest of helping those less fortunate. Anyway, it was enough for Justine to know that she was feeding the hungry and making the world a better place in her own small way.

Justine took over the cooking then, while Martha moved from table to table taking orders.

48 WHY NOW?

Josiah remained on her bed as he watched her stride away to face another long day of work. He was confused and mystified by what had just happened.

Why could she see me now? And she heard me, too. In all of the years I have been at her side, she has never shown any sign of recognition, but this morning. . .

He rose after spending several minutes in reflection and went to meet with William under the newly-repaired roof. Dangling Will had been dead for a very long time. Perhaps he would know the answer to the many questions that had arisen as a result of this morning's odd events.

"This is not good!" William rubbed his salt-and-pepper beard in a show of consternation. "Very few of the living are capable of that, and those skills are present from birth."

"Yet, I do believe she has heard me – on more than one occasion." Answered Josiah.

"And, me." Said William, with notable solemnity. "This can only mean one thing." He added, lifting his eyes to Josiah's.

"What? What are you trying to tell me, Will! Out with it, Man! I must have an answer or I'll shake it out of you – as God is my witness!"

William placed a hand on Josiah's shoulder and shook h is head, sadly. "She is dying, Josiah."

"Justine?" He laughed. "Why, that woman is a strong as a village mule!"

William dropped his hand from Josiah's shoulder and turned to look out of his window. "Nevertheless, she is dying. Only the dying and the very young can see or hear us, Josiah. That is the way of things."

"But she shows no signs of illness. . ." He ran both hands through his dark hair.

"Yet, death has her in its grasp all the same."

Suddenly, a guilty thought passed through him like an electric current.

Alive she is alone, but dead she can be mine forever!

"I see your wicked thoughts! How can you give them space to flourish! Would you have her wandering about this place with you for all eternity? Would you value your needs above hers? That is no love, Josiah. You should know better."

Josiah stood up to his full height and loomed over William with a storm of anger swirling in his eyes and muscles, bulging.

"You speak as though I brought the threat of death to her, myself! This is something that has come upon her naturally, for God's own reasons and in God's own time! Is it wrong to want to welcome her as she leaves all that is her life behind? Have I not proven my devotion to her?"

Will cringed under Josiah's display of outrage. "Yes. Yes. I apologize, Josiah. I know that this is not your doing."

Josiah wilted. "Is it too late? Can I warn her? Perhaps the doctors can. . . ."

"Her death must be imminent, or she would not have seen you."

"They can cure things these days, you know. I was at the hospital for weeks, and you wouldn't have believed the wonders I saw there."

"Tell her your concerns. She is a fighter, if ever there was one. But, she will have to be aware of the enemy if she is to have any chance to subdue it."

"I will. I will tell her the very moment I can get her alone."

"Good. That is the best we can do, Josiah. The rest is in God's hands."

49 CRYING OVER SPILLED MILK

Later that afternoon, as Martha had predicted, Mark showed up at the Granary asking for Justine. Though hardly ever caught away from the building, she was at that moment two blocks away buying milk, butter and bread for the café, and Martha told him as much.

"Well, I'll go ahead and get my tools and stuff from upstairs. She'll be back before everything can be loaded up."

"Sure. Go on up – Mark, is it? – I'm sure Justine wouldn't mind."

He nodded at Martha and started up the stairs.

As soon as Mark was out of sight, Martha dialed Justine's cell and let it ring until she picked up.

"Martha?"

"He's upstairs!" She whispered, loudly enough to get her message across, but not so loud that the dwindling lunch crowd could hear. "He's getting his stuff."

"Don't let him leave!! I'll be there in two minutes!"

"I'll keep him here if I have to jump on top of him and wrestle him to the ground!" She said, with more than a hint of lustful humor.

"Hey! He's my guy!" Justine countered. "At least, I hope he is. . ."

"Just hurry up and get back here!"

"I'm on my way!"

Justine was impatient with the cashier who was ringing up her purchases. As is usually the case, her obvious show of impatience only succeeded in slowing the obstinate employee to a slower crawl.

"There has been an emergency!" She said to the cashier. "I really need to go now! Can you please hurry up a bit?"

All she got for her trouble was the half-lidded eye roll that was reserved for only the most irritating customers.

"I'm sorry, Ma'am, but this is as fast as it gets. You're just going to have to wait, like everybody else."

Oh great. I should have just kept my mouth shut. Now, I'll be lucky to get out of here by nightfall. . .

As soon as Justine was free of the register, she shouldered her purse, scooped up the loops of all of the plastic bags in both hands, ditched her cart, and took off for the café.

My hair is a mess. She thought as she practically sprinted the couple of blocks to the granary. *Why did I have to go shopping today? I could have sent Martha to pick these things up. What was I thinking? Now, I probably won't even make it to the lady's room to freshen up a bit before he comes back downstairs!*

At that precise moment, one of the plastic loops ripped free and sent a gallon of milk skidding across the pavement at her side. The jug exploded dramatically, splashing her jeans and the hem of her shirt with milk and whatever grime it had managed to wash free from the cobblestones in the process.

Justine gained the sidewalk on the opposite side before stopping to survey the damage. Several choice words came to mind, but she just didn't have the energy to loose them on the neighborhood. Her shoes were squishy. Her right pants leg was soaked through, and any hopes she had of impressing Mark with her cool, elegant appearance slid away from her like a whipped dog.

I give up! She moaned, inwardly, as she step-squish-stepped her way to the café. *The guy didn't want me, anyway. I'll just pay him the money and bid him a fond 'fare-thee-well.'*

"What happened to you?" Martha had been waiting at the door to take some of the groceries.

"Don't ask. Just don't ask. I'm done. Who would give me a second glance in this condition?"

Taking the groceries from Justine's hands and placing them carefully on the counter, Martha shooed her upstairs.

"Go upstairs and change your clothes! He hasn't come down, yet, and when he does, I'll keep him occupied until you get back!"

"Martha, there's no time. It'll take me twenty minutes to look even remotely human again."

"Shh! Get up there and work some magic! Go on! Hurry up!"

50 LONG TIME, NO SEE

Justine slipped into her bedroom just in time to hear Mark struggling down the steps with something heavy and awkward. One glance in the bathroom mirror told her exactly what she had expected it to. She was a one-woman disaster area.

Tempted to give up and climb into bed, she somehow managed to rally enough to slip out of her soggy jeans, shirt, socks and shoes. Not knowing what else to do, she jumped into the shower and washed her hair – braiding it while it was still wet so that it hung neatly down her back.

Fresh clothes fought her every effort to button, zip or step into them, as clothing always seemed to do when there was no time for that sort of thing.

Justine blew into her hand and sniffed her breath. Nope. She was going to have to brush her teeth, too, if she didn't want to knock the man down where he stood.

In less time than she would have believed possible, she stood before the mirror once more, looking fresh and un-flustered. With a couple of well-placed pinches to bring color to her cheeks, she decided she would pass for cute, if nothing else, and descended with grace and dignity to the café to make her appearance.

"Ah! Now, that's much better!" Martha said as soon as she caught sight of Justine.

"Where is he?" Justine mouthed.

"Outside loading his truck."

"Oh."

"Now, get over here and look lovely, while I wash these dishes!"

"Yes, ma'am."

By the time Mark had come back inside to get his second load of tools from upstairs, Justine was standing on a chair, adjusting a particularly lovely painting of herself that was hanging high up on one of the far walls.

"Oh! There you are! I didn't know you had come back from the store."

"Mark! You're here just in time! Could you tell me if I've got this hanging straight? It seems to me that it is still leaning a bit too far to the left."

"Wait here! I've got a level in the truck."

Martha gave Justine the universally accepted sign for "OK!" as the door pulled shut behind him.

"You're better at this than I ever gave you credit for!" She said, causing one or two of the customers to snicker behind their hands.

When Mark returned he climbed up on the chair beside her and placed the level across the top of the frame. "You were right; a bit too far to the left. Here, bring it up just a bit on your end."

Doing as he asked, and brushing her hip against him in the process, they managed to secure the painting perfectly.

Mark helped Justine down off the chair and stood back to observe the painting. "That's you, isn't it?"

"Yes. It's one of my favorites, actually."

"You are gorgeous. The artist captured you beautifully."

"Thank you." She smoothed her blouse and batted her eyelashes. "I sometimes model to bring in extra money.

Justine watched Mark's face flush scarlet and knew what thoughts her statement had evoked.

"I can see what you're thinking, you naughty boy!" She whispered into his neck with a hot breath of air. "You're wondering if I've ever posed nude, aren't you?"

His color deepened several shades and he laughed, nervously. "You caught me."

"Of course, I have! Posed nude, I mean. There are several wonderful examples in my room. Would you like to see them?"

Mark coughed into his hand and shook his head.

"Maybe some other time." He choked.

"Oh. Are you in a hurry?"

"Well, I do need to get all of those tools loaded up and back to the shop." He started towards the stairs.

"Let me help you." She said, gliding provocatively up the stairs behind him.

51 SCARED OUT OF HIS MIND

Josiah followed the two of them up the stairs, shaking his head.

What does she think she's doing? Can't she see that the guy is scared out of his mind?

Anybody could see that this guy was not going to respond to an aggressive series of plays like those.

She'll be lucky to catch hold of his shirttails as he hot-foots it out of here!

Josiah had played all of the games during his lifetime, and had considered himself somewhat of an expert. Guys like this Mark person were all about laying down the moves and being in control of the game. All Justine had managed to do in the last few minutes was convince the guy he was out of his depth and needed to make a hasty retreat.

Women. He sighed.

"Pssst! Hey, you! Cleopatra!" He tapped her on the back with one finger.

"Go away!" She hissed.

"What?" Mark stopped to turn around. "Did you say something?"

She smiled broadly and waved him on. "Just shooing the cat." She answered. "I know you're allergic."

"Oh." He laughed, nervously and continued. "I am. Thanks for that."

Justine whirled to face Josiah. "What do you want?" She mouthed

"Stop it." He said, at full volume. (Nobody could hear him, anyway). "Can't you see you are scaring the poor boy to death?"

A crease formed between her brows as she considered his observation, then she turned to continue her ascent. From behind, Josiah saw her shrug her shoulders.

"Hang back a bit. Play it cool. You can take him or leave him. Got it?"

She slowed a bit and nodded her head.

"Besides, you don't need him, now that you have me." He reached out to tug on her braid, only to have her wave him away.

"I was surprised when you didn't show up for your check the other day. I was wondering what had happened to you."

Josiah winced. "Didn't I just tell you to back off?"

They reached the top landing and Mark busied himself winding power cords and placing parts into corresponding cases.

"Oh. Yeah. Sorry I didn't call."

"No problem."

Justine lifted two of the hard cases and started downstairs with them.

"Hey! Wait!"

"Huh?"

"Don't carry those! They're heavy. I'll get everything."

"Oh. Okay." She set the cases down. "Is there anything here that I can carry down?"

"Um." Mark casted about for something less dangerous and came up empty. "Not really. Thanks for offering, but. . ."

"Oh. Okay. Then, I'll just hand you this and get out of your way."

Mark stood there, looking at the check in her hand. On so many levels he knew that she couldn't afford the work he had done, and he truly felt awkward accepting the money.

"Look, Justine, if you want to just break this into payments. . ."

"No. No. I insist you take payment in full. I know this job would have cost three times as much anywhere else. I'm truly grateful for the cut-rate price you gave me." She hurried to add, "Cut-rate price for first-rate work!" so that he wouldn't take it the wrong way.

Hesitantly, he accepted the check, folded it in half, and slipped it into his shirt pocket. "Well, I'm glad I was able to help. Hope you'll call me if you need any work done in the future."

Now that the check was in his pocket and the awkward 'payment for services rendered' was out of the way, Justine felt herself becoming smaller. His comments were the kind a handyman said on his way out the door – not – as she had hoped – the flirtatious prelude to a dinner invitation.

"I told you so. . ." Josiah couldn't resist chiding from the sidelines. He instantly regretted it, though, as Justine merely hung her head and nodded in tacit agreement.

Mark started to scoop up equipment right and left, as though he felt he had to get it all in one trip.

"Well, I've got to get back to work. Don't try to move it all at once or you'll end up going down the hard way!" She joked, pointing to her pale arm.

"It was very nice meeting you, Mark. I promise to recommend you highly. Thanks, again."

She didn't remember anything after that; how she got to her bedroom; pulled off her fresh clothes, or climbed into bed. She didn't remember hearing him struggling up and down the rickety stairs with armfuls of equipment, the door closing behind him, or the truck starting up and pulling away. When Martha came upstairs to check on her, she was tear-stained and exhausted.

"Close early tonight, Martha. I'm just too tired."

"I think I could manage it . . ." Martha started to say.

"No. I want absolute quiet and I couldn't bear the guilt of having you pick up my slack."

When it had become clear that Justine would not be swayed in the matter, Martha walked around the room switching off the lights.

"Okay, honey. I'm just a phone call away, if you change your mind."

"Thanks, but I won't."

The words had been muffled by her pillows, but Martha got the message.

"Get some rest. I'll check on you in the morning."

There was no reply, so Martha showed herself out. She accepted payment where payment was offered, and told everybody that Justine was feeling ill and was going to close up early.

Knowing looks were exchanged between those who had noticed the speedy departure of the handsome workman.

The door was soon locked, the lights turned off, and all around her was darkness and silence.

I am being a brat; a childish brat, and I know it. She berated herself with her face still buried in her pillows. *I ruined everything, and now I'll never see him again. I am alone, and I am so tired! This place is too big, and it needs too much work, and I can't do it by myself anymore! Gabriel! I'm so sorry. . . It was our dream, together, but you left! I have tried! I have tried so hard! But, you are gone, and I am tired. . .*

"Knock – knock." Josiah said from the doorway.

"Go away!"

"I would. Any other time, I would, Justine. But, there is something important that we need to talk about; something quite urgent, actually."

"Can't you see I'm done for the day?"

"Justine . . ."

"God damn you, Josiah! Go away! I know that I made a total fool of myself! I know that I drove Mark out of my life, forever! Your input is not required! Now, get out!"

Figuring that he had done all he could do for the moment, Josiah settled in the corner of the next room and brooded. She had to know that something was terribly wrong. He had to tell her she was dying. . .

52 THE WEDDING THAT SET A SPIRIT FREE

February 23rd dawned clear and cold. Though snow drifts still lined the back streets and buried the occasional family car, the main roads had been plowed to the pavement and generously salted for days.

Kathy had already been laced, buttoned, zipped and hooked into all of her wedding finery, and was standing in front of the mirror in the Chapel's dressing room. Her hair had been braided and adorned with white silk rosebuds, and the veil that she had chosen hung just past her shoulders.

There had been so many dateless Friday nights, so many hurtful comments and rejections during her school years that Kathy had been afraid to dream of this moment – her wedding day. Yet, here she was, not just marrying the first person who showed an interest, but her true love and soul mate! She had experienced no periods of doubt, no fears for their future together. Billy had been the right man from the first moment.

As she primped and fluffed and made final adjustments to her dress and veil, Kathy found herself wondering whether or not their children would be gifted as they had been? How different would their childhoods be with parents that could also see, hear, and empathize with what they were experiencing? She vowed to use her abilities to help the living and the dead to find peace and direction where there had only been fear and confusion.

If everything went as planned during the ceremony today, they would be able to join together and bring peace to a tortured soul at the same time.

The organ music drifted into the room, and her maid of honor handed her the bridal bouquet. Everyone took their places; Kathy's mother at her side, as her father was not around to give her away. Joy filled her and the smile that resulted could have chased the shadows from the darkest room.

As they made their way down the aisle, Billy's eyes found hers, and there was a great love drawing them together for all to see.

Wow! She had never seen him in a suit, much less a tux. *Mr. Fische, you sure clean up nicely!*

Something pulled her eyes to the front row of pews that was reserved for family members. She almost stopped mid-stride when she saw him. The man with the poufy sleeves!

What is he doing here? Did he follow Justine?

Kathy put the smile back on her face and scanned the wedding guests for Justine. She found her, dressed to the nines and standing five rows back. They had both wanted her to be there. Kathy nodded a welcome to both Justine and the man with the poufy sleeves before fixing her gaze again on her future husband.

Never a dull moment. She thought with a

strange twist to her smile. *Ours will be an interesting life.*

"We have gathered here today to join this man and this woman in the bonds of Holy matrimony." Pastor Dave intoned. "Who will give this bride away today?"

"I will." Her mother, answered, smiling. Kathy thought she saw a tear trembling on the edge of her lashes.

Billy hugged his new mother-in-law and took Kathy's hand. His touch went through her like 250 volts, and, despite her best efforts, her knees began to tremble.

As the ceremony continued, everyone else seemed to melt away leaving the two of them alone with their vows. When Billy put the modest band on her finger, she felt like part of something wonderful; no longer alone in the world at all, but a part of something invincible.

"You may now kiss your bride!"

His arms swept her up with a strength she didn't know he possessed, and his kiss was full of the promise of things to come. The moment he released her from his embrace they joined hands and switched their focus to the next part. . .

Kathy crossed her fingers under the bouquet, and held her breath.

"Would everyone please remain seated?" Pastor Dave's voice rose above the clamor of the excited guests.

As everyone settled again into their pews, a lot of questioning looks were exchanged.

"Mr. and Mrs. William Fische would like you to stay and join with them in prayer for a dear friend who seeks forgiveness and healing from our Heavenly Father."

The room grew quiet.

"Let us pray."

Over a hundred heads bowed in prayer.

"Please repeat after me."

Kathy and Billy – hands still joined – bowed their heads.

"Heavenly Father, hear our prayer."

The wave of sound that echoed back to the pulpit was strong and resonant with the voices of men, women and children in attendance.

"We gather now to beg forgiveness for one of your lambs that went astray."

"Please grant safe conduct to William James Poston from his earthly prison to your eternal, healing light."

The prayer washed over them with such force that Kathy's knees threatened to give way.

"His heart has been overcome with remorse, and his penitent soul awaits your mercy."

"These things we pray, humbly, in the name of Jesus Christ, our Lord and Savior. Amen."

Kathy sought out Justine, and found her, crying,

in the fifth row. The man with the poufy shirt was nowhere to be seen.

"Please welcome, for the first time, Mr. and Mrs. William Fische!" Pastor Dave's announcement was jubilant, and managed to get everybody on their feet and cheering.

The couple raised their joined hands in the air and made their way, happily down the aisle to the applause of friends and family members. Both, happy to be man and wife; both hoping that today's efforts would set Dangling Will's spirit free to join his son on the other side of the light.

53 JOSIAH GETS THERE FIRST

Josiah had followed Justine to the wedding, because he followed her everywhere these days. She would not allow him to be anywhere near her since the day that Mark walked out of her life, and she still refused to listen to anything he had to say – be it urgent, or otherwise.

He had not planned to be drawn in by something as mundane as promises made by the living to honor and love one another until death. But, somehow, the young people – (the two that saw and heard what others could not) – were able to break through all of his defenses and touch his soul. If Justine had known anything about their plans to pray Will out of purgatory, she hadn't bothered to share it with him. To be quite honest, that part had come as a total shock.

That won't work. He had been certain. Nothing about God was ever that simple! *How childlike they are in their faith!*

But, as the prayer continued to resonate throughout the little chapel, it had shaken him – moved him to tears. . . The voices of so many; raised in supplication for one lost soul. . .

Could it work?

Suddenly, he had to know. In the same time that it would take for the couple to raise their hands to celebrate their union, Josiah was standing on the fourth floor of the granary. What he had found upon his arrival had brought him equal amounts of joy and sadness. For, there, against the wall that bordered the few yards of floor in which Will had spent the last two centuries, there was a wall of such brilliance that – had he still possessed the capacity to breathe – would have taken his breath away.

Once Josiah had become accustomed to the glare, he had been able to just barely make out the silhouette of his friend as he cowered, trembling, in front of it.

"Will?"

"Josiah! Judgment has come upon me at last. I am to be fed to the furnaces of hell where I will be consumed eternally by the flames and made to suffer the agony that never ceases!"

Josiah scratched his head and put his hands on his hips before dropping them, helplessly, to his sides. There simply was no satisfying some people. He shaded his eyes from the glare and tried to decide how best to handle this dilemma. On one hand, he would miss William's company a great deal, should he go off into whatever lay beyond that gaudy display of dazzling brilliance. . . On the other, well, it might be good to see him go free after so many decades of miserable penance. . .

"Will? Calm yourself. I don't think it's as bad as all that."

"Tell me that I don't have to go into it! I shouldn't have complained so bitterly about my fate! I am afraid, Josiah. Please, help me. There must be a way that I can stay here where I belong. I will vow to accept my imprisonment with grace from this day forward. How could I have been so foolish as to anger God to this extent? Help me to find a way, Josiah!"

Having spent most of his life as a bit of a cad, Josiah was tempted to play this for all it was worth. He smiled behind his hand and fought to contain his laughter.

"Do not look into it!" He commanded, with his most authoritative voice. "This is a very grave turn of events, and I shall have to think upon it for a while. Just promise me that you will not move from where you sit!"

"Oh, thank you, friend. I will remain in this spot for as long as it takes to make this foul portal close and leave me safely behind."

"Be brave, William. I shall return with the answers you seek, or not at all."

In the next instant, Josiah was rolling about on Justine's bed enjoying hysterical bouts of uncontained laughter.

Oh, the drama! He jumped to his feet to assume the pose of a hero delivering his sobering promise. *I shall return with the answers you seek, or . . . not . . . at . . . all!*

Josiah knew it was wicked of him to torture William, but he was also certain that Justine and the 'messengers' (as Dangling Will had called them) would be along shortly to clarify the matter, and it had simply been too rich of an opportunity to pass up.

There's no sin in having a bit of fun now and again, is there?

The bedroom rang again with the booming sound of his laughter.

54 A TIME FOR CELEBRATION

Though at least three people at the reception were anxious to see whether or not William Poston had been set free from his decades-long imprisonment at the granary, many more were in the mood to party. Billy's parents had sprung for a cash bar, and the D.J. they had hired was having no trouble getting people on the dance floor.

Tacks, nails and tape had been strictly forbidden in the church's reception hall, so the couple had chosen to fill the corners of the modestly-sized room with burgundy, white and pink balloons. Three-foot wide bands of white satin had been draped between each cluster of balloons to give the walls a more elegant appearance, and twelve round tables had been arranged around a parquet dance floor; each adorned with rich burgundy table cloths, a bouquet of white roses, white china and crystal stemware.

Both mothers had gotten together to decorate the twelve-foot expanse of rectangular tables reserved for the bridal party. They had placed white columns on either end with gorgeous tall bouquets on top, and had placed dozens of tiny candles among rose petals along the edge that faced the room. As a special touch, they had acquired several Victorian-era valentines that they placed at the apex of each loop of a burgundy sash that festooned the white table skirt.

Justine found Kathy and Billy shortly after their introduction into the reception hall and embraced them, warmly.

"I am just so touched by what you did for Will." She said. "And, on your wedding day, too!"

"Well, we did promise." Billy replied.

"I almost can't wait to go home and see if it worked!"

"Will you call us – no matter how late – and let us know?"

"I wouldn't interrupt your wedding night. . ."

"Please do! Please?" Kathy's eyes pleaded, sincerely. "We've been planning this for weeks, and hoping that it would work. Waiting another day would just about kill us."

"Well, alright, I guess." She laughed. "Okay. I promise to call. But, if you are . . . um . . . otherwise engaged. . . I'll just leave a message."

The couple shared a glance and laughed self-consciously.

"If it didn't work, tell him there are lots of other things we can try."

"You guys are just too much." Justine dabbed at her eyes.

"Hey. Are you okay?"

"Sure. Why?"

"You sort-of rubbed your side and sat down, earlier. It looked as though you were in pain?"

"Well, I probably was." She laughed. "I've been putting in a lot of hours on the 2nd floor renovations over the last few days. Once the last of the drywall is up, I can take my time over the taping and patching. I've just strained a muscle in my side. Those sheets are really heavy and awkward to work with." Justine pushed the tender spot on her side gingerly, and winced. "But, it is getting better every day. I'm sure it's nothing to worry about."

"You shouldn't be doing that kind of work by yourself." Kathy scolded. "What if you fall again, or break a hip or. . ."

"What? Hey. Breaking a hip is something senior citizens do! How old do you think I am, anyway?"

"You know that's not what we're saying." Billy slipped an arm around his bride's waist and stepped in. "Listen, when we get back from our honeymoon, I'll bring a couple of the guys over and see if we can help with the heavy stuff, okay?"

"That would be great!"

"In the meantime, why don't you stick to painting or something?"

"You sound like my mother!"

"Hey, friends look out for friends." Kathy took Justine's hand and pulled her in for a hug.

"Okay. You two get out there and mingle! I'm going to see if I can get one of those handsome bartenders to rustle me up a margarita."

"Don't forget!" Kathy called as they moved towards the dance floor, hand in hand. "You promised to call!"

As soon as the bride and groom were out of sight, Justine found a chair and sat down. She really hadn't been feeling well, lately. But, then again, if these spasms were something to worry about, surely it would have been discovered during her lengthy hospital stay? A disturbing recollection of Doctor Bauer's concern over her blood work tried to nudge its way through her wall of resolute optimism.

Watching the bride and groom make their vows to one another with their eyes alight and the love shining from in their faces had reminded Justine of her own girlhood dreams of a perfect wedding day – complete with Prince Charming. Sitting off to the side, completely alone, she allowed that dream to die. There was not going to be a white dress and veil in her future. That part of her life had been buried with her Gabriel, years ago.

She held the sweating goblet of ice water up in to her eyes and looked through it at the crowd of merry wedding-goers. The distorted lens seemed to melt the scene into a bright tableau of mixed colors, not unlike a Van Gogh or a Cezanne. A wan smile lifted the corners of her mouth and marked the vision's passing.

How long had it been since she'd thought about Gabriel? Had she ever actually stopped thinking about him?

A sharp pain wrenched through her side and

along her back, causing Justine to shift in her chair.

It's probably nothing. She assured herself; lifting the goblet to her lips.

55 A HAUNTING WOMAN

Mark Mattsen sat atop a nearly-finished roof in Abingdon. Recent heavy snowfalls and accumulations of ice had caused several older roofs to collapse, and though February was not the optimal time to be doing that kind of work, he had been happy to pull this assignment. Times being what they were, people were hugging their pocket change closer than their teddy bears, and he had already gone through the money he'd earned at the granary.

Damn.

There. He'd done it again. Trying to get through a single day without thinking about that place or that woman was proving to be a challenge.

Just let it go. He tried to shake it off. *She's got to be half crazy, living in that pile of rocks and lumber surrounded by cats.*

He pulled off his gloves, grabbed the bandana from the back pocket of his jeans, and wiped the sweat off his face. Seemed to him that no matter how cold it was outside, it was always hot as hell on the roof.

All she needs is the right man. Some guy who could lighten the workload, get her out of that dungeon for the occasional island get-away. Could I be that man?

As Mark scanned the job site, he mentally added up the time it would take to finish; deciding that he would hang tough and put in the additional two hours tonight rather than going through the hassle of weather-proofing the unfinished portion and coming back in the morning. With a heavy sigh, he tugged his gloves back on, shoved a stack of supplies over to the last corner and picked up his nail gun.

Like a chatty neighbor that shows up out of nowhere when you're unloading groceries and holds you hostage with all of the latest neighborhood gossip. That running dialog in his brain refused to shut up and leave him be.

But, I liked her. A lot. We had a sort-of 'connection' didn't we? And, she was smart, funny, (and, let's not forget – sexy).

The roof came together under his hands with an almost musical rhythm. Slide, scrape, bang, bang, bang – slide, scrape, bang, bang, bang. He had been doing this kind of work for so many years that it happened more as a reflex than a carefully-thought-out process. If he kept up this pace, he'd be done in one hour, instead of two.

She was okay. Yeah, she was sexy. But, sexy comes in all shapes and sizes. There's no shortage of sexy out there.

The nail gun needed to be re-loaded, and he did that as automatically as most people squeeze toothpaste on their toothbrushes at bedtime. He removed his gloves again to accomplish the re-load and made a snap decision to leave them off for a while.

Now, Tammy. That's a hot babe. She'd never have a cat. Hates the sight of them; thinks they're sneaky, or something like that. And, even if she did have a cat, she wouldn't let it piss and crap all over the damn place.

Slide, scrape, bang, bang, bang. Slide, scrape, bang, bang, bang.

Yeah. But Tammy is dumb as a dinner plate and just about as much fun to be around. She'd never think of feeding the homeless or picking up a nail gun, or. . .

Slide, scrape, bang, bang, bang.

Damnit!

A sliver of something sharp had found its way under Mark's fingernail, and it hurt like hellfire. Another few feet to lay down and he'd be out of there. He examined his finger and winced at the sight of the inch-long metal sliver that had embedded itself so deeply in the God Damned most painful place possible. He alternately shook his right hand and sucked on the finger. He had always made it a policy of his to refrain from using four-letter words on the job site, but the "f" bomb was right on the tip of his tongue.

Slide, scrape, bang, bang, bang. Slide, scrape, bang, bang, bang.

He finished the job before nightfall, and thought of nothing more after that than getting home and finding a pair of tweezers to dig that *pig-slapping-weasel-frying- fork-of-a-ship-sucking* metal beam out of his finger.

56 GIFT EXCHANGE

Justine called a cab and left the reception early with a lot on her mind. She hadn't been feeling well for a long time. There had been bouts of unexplained nausea, feelings of fatigue and even dizziness. Had she become so out of touch with her own needs that she'd failed to notice the warning signs of something significant?

As she watched the lights of the city reflecting off of icy surfaces like a watercolor landscape in motion, she soon became mesmerized. It had been a long day. A long year, come to that. Justine gathered her coat more closely around her and was soon fast asleep.

"Lady. Miss. We're here."

The cabbie's face had been a bit of a shock until she remembered where she was. He was painfully thin and his features seemed to rise from his skull like a craggy mountain range; deeply creased and weathered by the elements. She wondered when he had last eaten a full meal.

"Thank you. I must have fallen asleep. Long day." She had murmured by way of explanation.

"Your fare will be $35.00, please, Miss."

Justine thought he might be from India, but wasn't good at guessing people's origins. As she rummaged through her purse for the money to pay her fare, she made the decision to invite him in. She squinted at the small print under the photo that was posted on the back of the driver's seat.

Aravinda

"Here you go. . . Aravinda? Am I saying that right?" He folded the bills without counting them and slid them into his pants pocket.

"Yes, Ma'am."

"Brrr! It's really cold out tonight." Justine stepped out of the cab and pulled her keys out of her bag. "Would you like to come in for a minute, Aravinda? I own this café. Let me make you a sandwich and maybe some hot soup or coffee. Today's special was bean and ham soup. I can heat it up in a flash."

The man hesitated. He looked up and down the street, nervously, then back at Justine – sizing her up and ultimately deciding that she didn't look dangerous.

"That would be very good of you." He said. "I haven't had time to stop for a meal all day." Having decided to trust her, his face eased into a tired smile.

"No. I'm being selfish, really. I'm hungry, and I hate eating alone."

True to her word, the simple meal was laid out in a matter of minutes. The soup was thick and rich, with a comforting aroma that surrounded their faces with steamy warmth. Justine packed the driver's sandwich full of roast beef and cheese before toasting it into a melty and substantial meal. Having been less than truthful about her own hunger, she managed to pick at her much-smaller portion while he ate.

"Will you be driving all night, or are you done for the day?" She asked.

"I am taking fares, day and night, Ma'am. Whenever I am able."

"Oh! Please don't call me 'Ma'am'!" She laughed. "You can call me Justine."

"Ah. That I will do! It is nice to be meeting you, Justine."

"Are you from India?" She ventured a guess. "Your name and your accent sound Indian to me."

"Yes. I am here in the U.S.A. for only two years, so far. I am hoping to make enough money to bring my family over very soon."

"Your wife?"

"Yes; and I am also having two sons." At this, he reached into his back pocket to pull out a battered leather wallet; from which he produced a dog-eared photo of his family.

The photo showed a lovely woman in a Sari, with her arms circling two young boys.

"What a beautiful family! You must be very proud." She said, handing the photo back to him.

"I am missing them most horribly, Miss Justine. This has taken much longer than any of us had hoped."

His spoon scraped the soup bowl, and he wiped his mouth with his napkin. Justine removed his bowl and replaced it with a generous piece of pound cake.

"Oh! Miss Justine, Ma'am!" He put up both palms in protest. "I am eating too much that will put me to sleep!"

"Well, okay. You don't need to eat it right this minute." She removed the cake and busied herself wrapping it securely and putting it into a small paper bag. "Here; save it for later. I hope you like it. That's my grandmother's pound cake recipe. I made it this morning, so it is fresh and moist."

The cabbie hung his head as he accepted the bag from her. When he raised his eyes again, there were tears standing in them.

"Miss Justine, Ma'am. I was very hungry tonight. I was never so hungry in my life before. You are a kind woman who has given me more than food tonight. Do you know what I'm saying of you?"

Justine stepped up to Arvinda and wrapped him in a gentle hug. "And, I was lonely tonight. I was never so lonely in my life before." She said. "And, you have shared your time with me. So, we're even."

They said their goodbye's and she watched the cab pull away from the curb and drive off into the night. The dishes were gathered and left to soak in a sink full of suds.

Justine locked up, switched off the lights, and climbed the stairs to her room – too exhausted to think about the fate of William Poston, or Mark Mattsen, or her own tired self.

57 TIME TO WAKE UP

When Justine didn't come downstairs at 6:30 the next morning, Martha was concerned. She tried the cell number, but the phone had either lost its charge or been turned off, as her calls had gone straight to voicemail.

Okay. Here I go. Up these awful, wobbly, worm-eaten steps to fetch a grown woman out of bed for the third time in so many weeks.

Her knees had not been in good working order since the Clinton administration, and she hadn't moved into a rancher last year without good reason. But, even as she grumbled her way up to Justine's room, Martha knew she was more worried than annoyed. Justine was like clockwork; never late; and always in motion. Whether this recent malaise had come about as the result of psychological depression or physical illness, it needed to be addressed.

One of the (too many) kittens was crouched in a litter box on the first landing with a look of total concentration on its face and a twitching tail. Martha shook her head and continued up the second flight; grumbling to herself and huffing like a steam engine.

Those darn cats need to go! How many animals does one woman need?

Martha covered her nose and mouth with her hand in response to the thick, musky odor of urine-soaked fabric and centuries-old dust.

It's a wonder to me that girl hasn't expired from the stink!

Having reached the landing and taken a few minutes to catch her breath, Martha called out – tentatively – for Justine.

"Honey? Justine? Are you okay in there? It's

coming up on 7:00 a.m."

The quiet was wrong. Martha had a creepy feeling that made her want to return to the café and call somebody else to check on Justine.

"Justine? Are you okay in there? It's time to get up and get to work, lazy bones!"

An avalanche of garbage caused Martha to jump, whirl and grab her ample bosom in fear. The reflective eyes of Justine's black cat — (*What's that cat's name?*) — had been glowing back at her from the wreckage of the minor landslide, and Martha reached her boiling point.

"Shoo!" Martha's voice had gone up two octaves. "Shoo on out of here, you obnoxious creature! Lord have mercy! You like to scared me to death!"

Allowing her indignation to propel her forward, Martha stomped her way through the maze of cast-off items that kept curious folks away from Justine's room, and didn't stop until she had reached the light on Justine's bedside table. With an unusually loud "Click!"

the room came into better view, and Martha reached down to yank the blankets off of Justine with the same energy that she had used to strip the covers from her daughter, Emily, when she had refused to get up for school.

Immediately, Martha's worst fears were realized. There was something very wrong with Justine's color. Martha didn't have to touch the body to know that her eccentric friend had moved on to a better place at some point during the night.

"God rest her soul."

Martha leaned back against the dresser, then, and surrendered herself to tears.

In the doorway, Inky sat licking her right front paw. Tiger-Boy meowed balefully at the new human, and patted the empty food dish a few inches to his left with an air of significance.

It was time to wake up, and he was hungry.

58 HELLO AGAIN

With more than a little chagrin, Justine addressed the handsome man who had made himself, once again, comfortable in her bed.

"This is getting to be a bit of a habit with you, isn't it."

Josiah turned towards her and propped his head up on one hand. "I'd like for it to be more than a habit. What do you say we make it official?"

Justine laughed and moved to get out of bed.

It was a few moments before she noticed that something wasn't right. A quick glance behind her confirmed that suspicion.

"What have you done to me?" She demanded, staring at her body, curled peacefully, as though still asleep on the bed.

Josiah raised his eyebrows and shrugged. "Not me. I don't get to make the big decisions."

He could see the realization dawn on her face.

"I'm dead?"

He nodded.

"Dead, dead? Like 'Till death do us part' dead?"

He sat up and looked at his lap. "Yep."

"HOW DID THAT HAPPEN?" She yelled, angrily, with her hands placed firmly on her shapely hips.

"Well. . ." Josiah started.

"Never mind." She shook her head in frustration. It doesn't matter how it happened, does it? What matters is that I'm dead."

"Yep."

"I'm really, totally, and without a doubt. . ."

"Dead." He supplied, helpfully.

She dropped onto the bed beside him, drew her knees up to a kind of sitting fetal position, and buried her face in both hands.

"Who's going to open the café this morning? Who's going to finish the drywall and put the flooring down, and install the new sink and toilet that I just picked out. . ."

"Actually, you've just hit on a topic that I would like to address with you, when you're ready to discuss your future."

"My future?" She glared at him in disbelief. "What 'future' is that? Didn't we already establish the fact that I am deceased? Gone? Finished? Done?" That outburst complete, she dropped her face back into the cradle of her hands.

"Maybe I should have said 'our' future." He said after a time.

Some unintelligible mumbling emanated from her muffled face.

"I'm talking about you and me. 'Josiah and Justine;' The 'Bonnie and fricking Clyde' of ghosts."

She peeked at him with suspicion before unfolding her spirit to face him.

"We would stay here? Watch over the place? Moving in and out of the shadows for the next couple of centuries? Spying on people?"

"Well, I wouldn't have put it that way, exactly, but. . ."

She sighed her first ghostly sigh.

"I don't know." She pulled her hair back from her face and seemed to consider it.

What are my options?" She asked.

59 A FORK IN THE ROAD

With so much to get used to, and only two ghostly friends to discuss it with, Justine sought out her (until now) invisible friend from the fourth floor. She zapped to Will's earthly prison as though she had been getting around that way for years.

"Cool." She said, looking around for a spirit who fit the image of William Poston that she had created to match the sound of his voice.

"Oh, no!"

The words had come from a short-ish, plump-ish, graying man that was huddled on the floor in front of a wall of dazzling brilliance.

"Will?"

"You're dead!"

"Yeah. New development."

"Hey! Look, Will! It worked!" She exclaimed, pointing towards the overwhelming brilliance at his back.

"What worked?"

"Oh. That's right. You don't know, yet." She said, half to herself.

"Will? Do you remember Billy and Kathy? They came to talk to you one night?"

"Yes. The Messengers. I liked them." He smiled, in spite of himself.

"Well, they had this great idea to have their Pastor lead a special prayer of forgiveness for you – smack dab in the middle of their wedding ceremony!"

"In a church!"

"Yep." She nodded with encouragement,

pulling him to his feet. "And there were over a hundred people there. All praying together, right along with the Pastor."

"For me?" Will was now standing.

"And, look! It worked, William! You've been forgiven! The light has come for you!"

Will's brows knit with consternation as his eyes went from Josiah to Justine to the wall of light and back again.

"Ha." Josiah stepped up to slap Will on the back. "That's right, old friend! I was just kidding around, earlier. Never could resist an opportunity to pull somebody's leg. . ."

Angry now, but still not certain which story to believe, William stood facing the wall of light.

"Is my son in there, do you think?"

Justine and Josiah exchanged looks and shrugged.

"We've never been through it." Josiah said.

"But, whatever's in that place has got to be better than being stuck in here."

"How do I know it isn't just a shortcut to Hell?" Will asked nobody in particular.

The three spirits shifted from foot to foot considering Will's dilemma.

"Well, for starters," Justine ventured "that light didn't show up until a whole crowd of people offered up a prayer of forgiveness for your soul."

Will seemed to consider her point, carefully. But, he still wasn't convinced.

"I know!" Josiah exclaimed. "Can you move freely around the building now?"

"I haven't tried, but."

"So? Try!" Josiah urged. "Walk over to the stairs and back. If you are still locked into this corner, then you are still imprisoned."

"That makes sense to me, Will." Justine said. "I think you should give it a go. Would you like me to walk with you?"

"No. No. This is something I need to do on my own." Will wrung his hands, nervously as he spoke. "But, thank you; and you, too Josiah. I believe you're right about this state of affairs. I'm either free to choose – as you have always been, Josiah – or . . ." Will gulped.

"Go ahead." Justine urged.

"Yes. Do." Josiah echoed, moving to give William a clear path to the stairwell.

Will stopped at his usual boundary out of habit, and looked back at his friends for encouragement.

"Go ahead!" They chimed in unison.

The next stride took Will through his customary boundary and beyond. Once he had reached the stairs and started back, Justine and Josiah cheered and applauded.

"I'm free." Will whispered. "The Messengers kept their promise."

Tears ran freely down his face and sobs shook his ghostly form.

"What's the matter, Will? Aren't you happy to be getting out of here?"

"I want to be. I do." He whispered through his tears. "But, I'm still afraid! I'm afraid to walk through there alone."

The three of them stood there, side by side, bathed in the brilliant light of the beckoning unknown; each at a major fork in the road and unsure of which path to take.

ABOUT THE AUTHOR

Kaye Giuliani is the Founder of Proof Finders Paranormal Investigations. Check out the website at: (www.prooffindersparanormal.com)!

She lives in Odenton, Maryland, with her husband and their faithful dog, "Milky." A mother of three married children and a cancer survivor of just over three years, Kaye is determined to write books that show ghosts in a better light.

"Grains of Truth" is book three of the "Charity Fish" series. If you enjoyed this book and haven't read the first two: "Charity Fish," and "The Farmer Takes a Child," then please do! Also, consider writing a favorable review on Amazon.com!